Business Law Basics

Margaret E. Vroman

Northern Michigan University

Kendall Hunt
publishing company

Kendall Hunt
publishing company

www.kendallhunt.com
Send all inquiries to:
4050 Westmark Drive
Dubuque, IA 52004-1840

ISBN 978-0-7575-6338-6

Printed in the United States of America
10 9 8 7 6 5 4 3 2

Dedication

This book is dedicated to my mother who always believed I would someday write a book—although I don't believe this is exactly what she envisioned.

Contents

Chapter 14   Criminal Procedure   85

Chapter 15   Real Property   93

Chapter 25   Agency   157

Chapter 26   Landowner Duty of Care   167

Chapter 27   Landlord Tenant Law   171

Chapter 28   Intellectual Property

Chapter 1
Introduction to Law

Introduction

Every person in the United States comes into contact with the legal system in one way or another. If you buy or sell a house, challenge a speeding ticket in court, sign a contract as a condition of starting a new job, or return a cell phone because it doesn't work, you are dealing with the U.S. legal system.

Knowledge of our legal system is essential because it is this mechanism that helps us resolve conflicts, punish individuals who violate the law, and solve many of society's problems. This text provides information on the fundamentals of the U.S. legal system, the mechanics of the legal process, and an overview of numerous substantive areas of law. Real-life cases are included to demonstrate how this system works, and hypothetical questions are included to challenge students' critical thinking skills and assess their overall comprehension of the subjects covered.

Types of Law

There are two types of legal systems in use in most of the world. The most common legal system is the civil law system. It grew out of Roman law, Canon law (church law), and other religious laws. France, Germany, Switzerland, as well as other European countries and their colonies, use the civil law system, which is based on codes or written laws that judges apply to individual cases. Judges in the civil law system apply these codes to the cases that come before them.

Great Britain, however, differed from its European neighbors by developing and using what has come to be called the *common law legal system*. Because the United States was originally a British colony, it also uses the common law legal system.

The common law legal system creates legal rules from the facts of specific cases and applies those rules to other cases with similar facts. The rules may "evolve" as time and the facts presented to the court change. This precedent-based process is different from the civil law system, which starts with the rules and then has judges apply them.

Although the United States uses the common law legal system, it also has codes (statutes) that the courts apply. When a case is presented, the court first determines if there is a statute that applies to the facts of the case. If no statute applies, then the court looks to previous cases for a rule it can apply. In the common law system, judges have the authority and duty to make legal rules by interpreting the law of earlier cases or creating new and precedential rulings.

Precedent is the common law system's use of rulings rendered in previous legal cases. The body of precedent (legal rules established by previous decisions) is called *common law*, and it binds future decisions. When parties disagree on what the law is, a court will look at past decisions and the precedents they have established and apply them to the facts of the case currently before it. The judge may take an existing rule of law and its rationale and use it to craft a new rule, which then becomes precedent for the cases that come after it. Under the common law system, if a similar dispute has been resolved in the past, the court is obligated to follow the reasoning and rule used in the earlier case. This principle is known as *stare decisis*, which is Latin for "let the decision stand."

If, however, the court finds that the current dispute is fundamentally distinct from all previous cases, it will decide the case as a "matter of first impression." This means the issue is the first time the court has been presented with it. Once the court makes a ruling on this issue, its decision becomes the rule, or precedent, and will bind future courts under the principle of *stare decisis*.

Common law systems are more complicated than civil law systems. The decision of a court is binding only in its particular jurisdiction, and even within a given jurisdiction some courts have more power than others. A court's jurisdiction is the geographical area over which it has authority. It is also the subject matter over which the court has authority.

Interactions between common law, constitutional law, statutory law, and regulatory law also make understanding the U.S. legal system difficult. However *stare decisis*, the principle that similar cases should be decided according to similar rules, lies at the heart of all U.S. court decisions.

Sources of Law

There are four sources of law in the U.S. legal system. These are: the U.S. Constitution, statutes (and ordinances), common law, and administrative or regulatory law.

The Constitution

Although the U.S. legal system is based on common law, unlike Great Britain, it also has a constitution. The U.S. Constitution is a document adopted by the country's founders and designated as the supreme law of the land. It establishes the principles of government upon which the United States is governed. Individual states may also have constitutions, but the U.S. Constitution is superior to all state constitutions and state and federal laws. The Constitution divides the country's governing powers between the federal government and the states. It details specific powers that only the federal government has. For example, it states that only the federal government has the right to establish a military. Because of this, there can be no state militias.

Statutes and Ordinances

Statutes and ordinances are legislation (laws) passed at the federal, state, and local level. As long as a state law is not preempted by or contradicted by a federal law, a state is free to pass its own laws.

Common Law

Common law is based on precedent, in which the facts of the case before the court are compared to those of previous cases having similar facts. The rule of law applied in the earlier case is applied to the current case and perhaps modified a bit to deal with the new situation.

Common law has the ability to evolve as technologies and society change, and it offers a predictable and stable form of law around which commerce can thrive. The criticism of common law is that it may result in judge-made law when judges fail to honor the principle of *stare decisis*. When this happens it may lead to unpredictable and unfair applications of law.

Administrative Law

Administrative law is the legislation (in the form of rules and regulations) passed by administrative agencies for the purpose of carrying out the intent of the law that created the agency. For example, the Environmental Protection Agency was created by federal statute and given certain duties concerning the protection and preservation of the environment. This statute also gave the agency the authority to create its own regulations to help it carry out its duties.

Priorities in Law

The U.S. system of government is also unique because it recognizes both a federal system of laws and the ability and right of individual states and local governments to make their own laws. Because of this, U.S. citizens are subject to the laws and rules of several different entities at the federal, state, and local levels.

Naturally, there is a priority in the application of these laws, and if there is a conflict between them, the higher law is controlling and will be applied. In some instances, the court will rule that a lesser, conflicting, law is invalid. The priority of laws is as follows:

1. The U.S. Constitution
2. Federal statutes
3. State constitutions
4. State laws
5. Local laws
6. Common law (not codified)
7. Administrative (regulatory) law

The U.S. Constitution

Because the U.S. Constitution is the "supreme law," no state may make a law that conflicts with it. Under the Constitution, any power that is not specifically given to the federal government by it is reserved to the states. Similarly, powers that are not specifically reserved by states in their constitutions may be exercised by local governments.

When the Constitution or a federal statute gives the federal government sole control over an area, it "preempts" the states from passing any law in that area. For example, because the Congress has passed a law giving the federal government control over immigration issues, no state may pass a law that attempts to regulate immigration.

The Constitution also grants Congress the right to make laws that it deems "necessary and proper" to carry out the powers granted to it by the Constitution. This implied power gives Congress wide leeway in making laws.

Federal Laws

When a bill is passed by the United States Congress, it becomes law and part of the U.S. Code. The U.S. Code (USC) contains public laws that are applicable to all U.S. citizens. Federal regulations, which are like laws, are adopted by executive agencies and are contained in the Administrative Procedures Act. They are codified in the Code of Federal Regulations (CFR), which is also an important source of federal law.

State Constitutions

Every state in the United States of America has adopted its own constitution. Both federal and state constitutions provide for the legal and political organizations of their respective sovereign entities. However, while the U.S. Constitution prescribes the limits of federal power, state constitutions describe the structure and process of those governmental powers that are not delegated to the federal government. Many state constitutions also address specific issues that its legislature determined were of sufficient importance to be included in the constitution rather than a statute. As long as a provision in a state constitution does not contradict the U.S. Constitution, it is enforceable.

State Laws

States are free to pass laws that do not conflict with the U.S. Constitution or federal laws, and they may regulate any area the Constitution leaves to them. Sometimes a federal law may regulate part of a subject area without preempting the entire field. If this happens, a state may pass some laws on the subject but not those prohibited by the federal law. A federal statute may explicitly state that it is preempting an area of law and preventing states from enacting their own, but often it does not. In such instances, the courts must decide whether the area has been preempted or whether a state has the authority to pass laws on the subject.

If the court determines a state law is in conflict with a federal law, it will rule that the federal law preempts that of the state. However, if an area is not preempted, there may be both a federal and a state law on the same subject. The federal law will apply when federal courts have jurisdiction over the parties and the state law will govern when the state has jurisdiction. If preemption is not an issue, a state may pass a law that is more restrictive than a federal law but it cannot pass a valid law that is broader than a federal law. For example, if a federal law states that no skyscraper may be more than sixty stories tall, no state can enact a valid law that allows skyscrapers to be seventy stories tall. However, a state may pass a law that says no skyscrapers may be built within its boundaries that are more than fifty stories tall. If, however, the entire subject of skyscraper construction were preempted by federal statute, a state could not pass any law concerning the construction of skyscrapers.

Just as the U.S. Constitution specifies certain areas where the federal government preempts state government authority, a state constitution may specify areas where its authority preempts that of local governments.

The Constitution also leaves the states in charge of certain things. It does this is by saying that any authority not given to the federal government may be exercised by the states. Because it doesn't specify what these areas are, the courts are left to interpret what the Constitution's drafters intended.

Every state has its own separate government with its own constitution. As such, each state has the power to make laws covering anything that is not preempted by the U.S. Constitution or federal statute. Many states have legal codes, just as the federal government has. Codifying laws passed by the legislature was adopted from the civil law system. Thus, our legal system uses both the common law principal of precedent and the civil law method of codifying statutes or laws.

Louisiana is the only state that does not base its legal system on common law. This is because Louisiana was originally settled by the French, who followed the French civil code system of law.

Local Laws (Ordinances)

An ordinance is a law made by a city, county, or other local government. Just as the federal government has left certain law-making authority to the states, the states have left certain law-making authority to local governments. This authority usually entails the power to pass laws governing property and conduct within the local government's geographical boundaries. These laws, or *ordinances* as they are called, are valid so long as they don't conflict with state or federal laws or constitutions. Much of what local government ordinances regulate is the use of land (zoning) and permits for such things as building construction or outdoor activities. These ordinances are subject to judicial interpretation, just like their federal and state counterparts.

Civil and Criminal Law

There are two types of laws that legislatures pass: civil laws and criminal laws.

Civil Law

Civil law regulates the rights and duties of, and between, individuals. It encompasses both the substance of laws regulating the rights and duties between individuals, as well as the process of judicial proceedings involving lawsuits between private parties.

Criminal Law

Criminal law regulates and punishes individuals for conduct that is offensive to society as a whole. It involves the prosecution of wrongful acts that are considered to be so serious that they are a breach of the government's peace, which cannot be deterred or remedied by lawsuits between private parties. The result of a criminal conviction is often incarceration in jail or prison. Incarceration is not a remedy available in civil cases.

Most crimes committed in the United States are prosecuted and punished at the state level. Federal criminal law focuses on areas unique to the federal government, such as a failure to pay federal income tax or interstate crimes like drug trafficking and wire fraud.

All states have somewhat similar laws regarding the most serious crimes, although penalties for these crimes may vary from state to state. Some states distinguish between two levels of crimes: felonies and misdemeanors. Felonies are the most serious criminal offenses, murder, rape, or robbery. Felony convictions result in longer prison sentences as well as probation, fines, and orders to pay restitution to victims. Misdemeanors are less serious criminal offenses—simple assault, drunk driving, or disturbing the peace—and typically result in less than a year in jail and/or a fine.

Depending on the conduct at issue, it is possible for a person to be charged both civilly and criminally as a result of a single action. For example, if a person commits an assault and battery against another person, the person may be sued civilly *and* prosecuted criminally. The civil case compensates the injured person (victim) for such things as medical bills, pain and suffering, and lost wages while the criminal case punishes the perpetrator for conduct that negatively impacts society or the state. The civil case compensates the injured party, and the criminal case deters similar conduct and punishes the perpetrator.

Cause of Action

Whenever one party sues another in court by filing a civil lawsuit, it must state a legal cause of action that entitles the party to proceed. It is possible that it will have more than one cause of action, but without at least one, the judge will dismiss the case.

The *cause of action* is the facts and legal theory that give a person (the plaintiff) the right to seek judicial redress or relief against another (the defendant).

It is the cause of action that is stated in the plaintiff's complaint, which is the initial pleading that starts a lawsuit. It is not sufficient merely to state that certain events occurred and that the plaintiff is entitled to compensation because of them. All the elements of each cause of action must be detailed in the complaint, along with facts that support it. The plaintiff must state the legal theory that entitled the plaintiff to the relief sought and must apply this law to the facts being alleged.

The cause of action is often stated by use of deductive reasoning that begins with a major premise (the applicable rule of law), proceeds to a minor premise (the facts that gave rise to the claim), and ends with a conclusion. For example, in a cause of action for battery, the rule of law is that any intentional, unpermitted act that causes a harmful or offensive touching of another is a battery. This is the major premise and would be stated first. Supporting facts, constituting the minor premise, would appear after the rule of law. Typically, a statement of fact for a case of battery might be, "The plaintiff, while walking through Sam's Grocery Store on the morning of January 2, 2010, was tackled by the defendant, a security guard for the store, who knocked the plaintiff to the floor and held him there by kneeling on his back and holding his arms behind him. These actions caused the plaintiff to suffer injuries to his head, chest, shoulders, neck, and back." The cause of action would conclude with a statement that the defendant is responsible for the plaintiff's injuries and that the plaintiff is entitled to compensation from the defendant.

The facts or circumstances of a situation may create more than one cause of action. For example, in the preceding example, the plaintiff might assert claims for assault, battery, intentional infliction of emotional distress, and a violation of his civil right. He might also bring claims for negligent hiring if the guard had a history of violent behavior that the store failed to discover, or for negligent supervision. When damages are caused by an employee, it is common to sue both the employee and the employer. All these causes of action arise from the same set of facts and circumstances but are supported by different rules of law and constitute separate claims for relief.

A cause of action can arise from an act, a failure to perform a legal obligation, a breach of duty, or a violation of a legal right. The importance of the act, failure, breach, or violation lies in its legal effect and in how the facts and circumstances, considered as a whole, are governed by applicable law. A set of facts may have no legal effect in one situation, whereas the same or similar facts may have significant legal implications in another situation. For example, tackling a shoplifting suspect who is brandishing a gun is a legitimate action by a security guard and would not support a claim for battery if the suspect were injured as a result. By contrast, tackling a shopper who merely acts in a suspicious manner and who the security guard thinks may be shoplifting is an inappropriate exercise of the guard's duty and may well give rise to several causes of action.

Real Life Case—Preemption

California passed a law prohibiting the importation or sale within California of products made from kangaroos. In the case of *Viva! International Voice for Animals v. Adidas Promotional Retail Operations Inc,* 162 P. 3d 569 (2007), Adidas Corporation conceded it was violating this law but argued that the federal government's policies concerning the international management of kangaroo populations preempted California's power to regulate the importation or sale of kangaroos.

The California court rejected Adidas's argument and upheld the California law on the ground that no conflict existed between state and federal policies or law in this area. The court analyzed the federal Endangered Species Act (ESA) and concluded the law was intended to protect endangered and threatened species from depletion and possible extinction. The Court said because kangaroos have at times been listed as threatened species, the ESA did not prevent California from regulating the importation of non-endangered species.

However, Adidas argued that kangaroo regulation is the unique province of federal authorities and that because the U.S. government had been working with Australia to develop effective kangaroo management practices, California could not interfere with or contradict federal policies.

Adidas contended that the federal government made an explicit decision not to ban kangaroo importation into the United States as part of an agreement with Australian national and regional governments. In exchange, Australia promised to regulate excessive kangaroo destruction.

The California court rejected this argument and instead relied on the "joint cooperative state–federal approach to wildlife preservation" it found to be reflected in a preemption provision contained in the ESA itself. Although a section of the ESA does purport to preempt state laws that permit what the ESA and its implementing regulations expressly prohibit, or prohibit what the ESA and its implementing regulations expressly permit, it also says the ESA "shall not otherwise be construed to void any State law or regulation. . . ." and that "any state law or regulation [concerning] endangered species or threatened species may be more restrictive than the exemptions or permits provided for in [the ESA] but not less restrictive than the prohibitions so defined." *Viva! International Voice for Animals v. Adidas Promotional Retail Operations Inc,* **162 P. 3d 569 (2007)**

The court reasoned that this provision gives states the power to regulate threatened animals like kangaroos that are not currently listed as endangered.

Even if the California court is right that the ESA does not support preemption, the state court decision might still be reversed because of the agreement the United States made with Australia. Because the Constitution gives the federal government (and the president) the power to negotiate with foreign countries and foreign companies, California's law could be declared unconstitutional by the U.S. Supreme Court.

Chapter 2
Court Organization

Introduction

The U.S. court system differs from that used by other countries in a number of ways. Our unique system of government recognizes the authority of not only the federal government but also the individual states that make up the United States of America. Because of this dual authority, the United States has both federal and state courts. This parallel system of courts can be a bit confusing, but the Constitution establishes the federal court system as superior to that of the states, and it makes the U.S. Supreme Court the highest court in the country at the top of the federal court system. The Supreme Court's decisions are final and cannot be appealed or overturned by any other court. Because it is the highest court in the country, its decisions are binding precedent on all courts dealing with any aspect of federal law.

Underneath the U.S. Supreme Court are the federal appellate courts, which hear and decide cases from the federal district courts. There are thirteen judicial circuits, each with its own court of appeals.

Beneath the appellate (circuit) courts are the federal district courts, which are the courts that hear evidence and conduct trials. They are the courts that use juries and make the initial rulings and decisions on a case. It is the decisions from these courts that may be appealed to the circuit court and possibly the U.S. Supreme Court.

Typically, a case starts in a trial court, where evidence and witnesses are presented before a judge or jury, who decides the case. An appellate court hears appeals from parties who claim that the trial court made a mistake in interpreting or applying the law. The appellate court rules on questions of law, not questions of fact. It does not review the evidence in a case or retry the case, but considers only legal issues. If it determines that the trial court judge made an error in interpreting or applying the law, it may reverse the decision of the trial judge or send the case back to the trial judge to reconsider based on its rulings. If it sends the case back to the trial court judge, it is *remanded* for action consistent with the appellate court's decision. If the appellate court agrees with the trial court and does not find any errors or mistakes, it will *affirm* the lower court's decision.

The state court systems deal with most of the issues affecting everyday life, such as marriage and divorce, real estate, and criminal law. Federal courts deal mostly with cases interpreting federal laws or involving parties residing in different states. There is some overlap in the types of cases federal and state courts consider, especially in such areas as environmental law and labor relations.

The effect of a court decision depends on the level of the court that issued the decision. The decision of an appellate court is binding precedent on all lower courts in its jurisdiction. The effect of a district court decision is only binding on that particular court since it is not an appellate court and has no authority over any other court.

Sometimes a court is asked to decide a legal question that no other court in its jurisdiction has ruled on before. When there is no precedent for the court to rely on, the case is referred to as a *case of first impression*. This is because it is the first time a court has been asked to rule on the question and its decision will establish the rule and precedent for that issue in all future cases. In these instances a court may review decisions on the issue from courts outside its jurisdiction, even though such decisions are not binding. These decisions may still provide legal references and rationale the court wishes to adopt in making its decision.

The Federal Court System

Apart from specialized courts, the federal court system comprises the following:

The Supreme Court of the United States	The Supreme Court hears cases appealed from federal circuit courts and from state supreme courts that involve an issue of federal law. The court has discretion to choose which cases it will consider.
U.S. Courts of Appeals (also called Circuit Courts of Appeals)	These appellate courts decide cases appealed from federal district courts in their circuits.
U.S. District Courts	District courts are trial courts that decide cases involving violations of federal civil and criminal law, treaties, or cases between residents of different states.

State Court Systems

Each state establishes its own judicial system so there are many variations, but most state systems are similar to the Michigan court system, described here:

Type of Court	Function	The Michigan Court System
Court of last resort (usually called the Supreme Court)	This court decides appeals from lower courts. It has discretion to choose which cases it reviews.	The Michigan Supreme Court is the court of last resort for the state of Michigan.
Intermediate appellate courts	Appellate courts hear appeals from lower (trial) court decisions.	In Michigan, the court of appeals is divided into four districts. They consist of twenty-eight judges who sit on three judge panels.
Trial courts	Trial courts conduct trials at which evidence is heard in both civil and criminal cases.	Each county has a circuit court with specialized divisions by subject, which deal with criminal felony cases and civil cases over $25,000. There is at least one district court in each county that deals with traffic cases, misdemeanor criminal cases, and civil cases involving less than $25,000.

Chapter 3
Litigation

Introduction

When parties cannot solve a legal disagreement themselves, they may resort to filing a lawsuit in court, where a judge or jury will render a decision on the matter, which they can enforce. The process of filing a lawsuit to achieve a decision in a civil matter is referred to as *litigation*. Litigation is one way that people and companies resolve legal disputes arising out of all sorts of factual circumstances. Not all disputes are subject to resolution by the courts, however. Courts can only decide cases involving disputes that involve a legal violation, not a dispute where the conduct alleged is merely a moral violation.

Moral disputes involve behavior that may or may not be a violation of religious rules for behavior. Moral rules are used when deciding whether conduct is good or bad. Some moral laws have been codified by governments and are legally enforceable. However, there are some moral rules that people may believe the law should enforce, but it does not. For example, Sam tells Sally his birthday is Friday and she buys him a present and gives it to him on Friday, thinking it is his birthday. If Sam lied and his birthday is not on Friday, does Sally have a right to take back the present Sam wrongfully induced her to buy? Most courts would say no. Although Sam's conduct is "wrong," the law does not recognize a legal cause of action on the part of Sally to get back the present she gave him based on his lie. Although lying in this instance may be a violation of a *moral* rule, the law does not recognize a person's right to have a court determine a remedy in this instance—or many other instances where someone has told a lie. The law requires that several other circumstances be present before a lie can be the basis of litigation.

Laws enacted by legislative bodies are intended to govern the behavior of individuals, businesses, and the government, but they do not regulate every aspect of behavior, nor are they intended to. If a party attempts to have a court decide a question that does not involve a legally recognized right or cause of action, the case will be dismissed—even if it involves the violation of a moral rule.

However, when a person or organization seeks to have a court determine if another has violated a legal duty owed that party, the party may exercise its constitutionally guaranteed right to trial.

Deciding to Go to Trial

Not all instances where the violation of a legal duty is alleged end up in litigation. A party should examine the amount of money at stake and balance it against the cost of litigation and the probability of success.

A major portion of the decision of whether to go to trial and have a judge or jury decide contested issues involves a cost–benefit analysis. If the financial benefit that may be received from going to trial is higher than the cost of going to trial, it may make sense to go to trial. However, it is not uncommon for attorney fees, court costs, and expert witness fees to be more costly than the amount likely to be awarded, even if the party is successful in court.

If the parties disagree over the amount of compensation one of them is due because of the failure of one party to deliver goods as required under their contract, and the difference in their valuations is substantial, then it might make sense to let a judge decide what the dollar amount of damage the contract breach caused. But if the amount of money at issue is $10,000, and it will likely cost $20,000 to go through the trial process, the party disputing the $10,000 in damages will end up spending more than what it will gain even if it wins in court.

Therefore, before deciding to go to trial, a party should look at the facts of the case objectively. It should be realistic about how the facts will appear to a neutral observer. Too often, emotion and ego cause a party to engage in fruitless litigation. Setting aside emotions and assessing the following will result in a much more rational result.

Factors to Consider before Deciding to Litigate

1. **What are the financial costs of the litigation?**
   - What are the legal fees and costs?
   - What are the costs associated with public relations issues?
   - What are the costs resulting from disclosing pending litigation?
   - What are the costs of alternatives to litigation?
   - What are the costs of not litigating?

2. **What public relations issues are involved in the litigation?**
   - What aspects of the litigation might interest the media?
   - What aspects of the litigation might produce strong emotions (either positive or negative) in a jury?
   - How might litigation affect company shareholders, competitors, and customers?

3. **What legal precedents are relevant to this litigation?**
   - Are there any legal precedents directly on point that make success in litigation extremely unlikely or extremely likely?
   - Are there precedents that might be available, although they do not directly apply to this litigation?

4. **What factors affect the possibility of settlement?**
   - Who is the opposing attorney or law firm?
   - How complex are the legal issues?
   - Are there other legal proceedings involving the same issue?
   - What are the weaknesses of the opponent?
   - What are the weaknesses of our position?

5. **Are there company policies that are relevant to this litigation?**

6. **What are the chances of getting help from other businesses in this litigation?**

Managing Costs

If a company decides that litigation is in its best interest, it must then take steps to manage its litigation costs. To do this it should consider the following:

1. **What will the attorney costs be?**
   - What is the hourly rate for the lawyer or lawyers involved?
   - How much assistance will the lawyer(s) need, and what are the hourly rates for those who will be assisting them?
   - What types of expert witnesses will be needed, and how much will it cost to have those experts prepare and testify?
   - What types of costs and fees will be involved (e.g., court fees, depositions, trial transcripts, and other discovery costs)?

2. **How much money is likely to be recovered if the litigation is successful?**
   - How much money is at issue in this dispute?
   - What is the financial condition of the potential defendant?
   - Where is the defendant located? Is the defendant in our state or in another state? (If the defendant is in a different state, costs of collecting the judgment are likely to be much higher.)
   - What reputation does our company wish to maintain?
   - What publicity is this action likely to cause?
   - What is the public's perception of the issues likely to be?

3. **How will the litigation affect relationships with government agencies and regulators?**
   - Would settling the case be in the company's best interest in this instance?
   - What is our ongoing relationship with this regulator?
   - What relationship do we wish to have with the government? How will this action affect that relationship?
   - Does this action involve a new regulation? Is the agency likely to use our company's case as a test case?
   - Are other companies involved or likely to be involved in this action? If so, might they help us in the suit?
   - What is the nature of the regulatory environment involved in this action? How is the current environment likely to affect our case?

The Trial Process

If a party decides to litigate a legal issue, it can be a lengthy and costly process. Although the steps may vary between the federal and state process, and between states, the following is a typical example:

1. A complaint alleging at least one cause of action is filed against the defendant(s).
2. Defendant answers the complaint by admitting or denying the allegations made.
3. Depending on the jurisdiction, mandatory arbitration or mediation may be required.
4. Discovery to obtain information from the opposing party is conducted.
5. A pretrial conference establishing time frames and dates is conducted.
6. Motions may be heard (at any time).
7. Trial is conducted and a judgment rendered.

Hypothetical Case

Sam's Produce Company has a contract to supply Sally's Grocery Store with 100 bushels of fresh potatoes every week. The price Sally's is to pay for the 100 bushels of potatoes is stated as "market rate." Sally's Grocery Store advertises the fact that much of its produce, such as Sam's potatoes, is locally grown. Customers seem to prefer buying locally grown produce. Sam's costs continue to rise, so he tells Sally he will begin charging $1.00 a bushel more for potatoes, beginning with the next delivery. Sally tells Sam that is too much. Thinking Sally won't pay any more, and getting angry, Sam contacts a newly opened grocery store and offers its potatoes at $0.50 more than Sam's Produce Company is currently getting from Sally's Grocery Store. The new store agrees to buy 100 bushels a week at that price. Sally then contacts Sam and says her store will pay him $0.50 a bushel more for his potatoes but not $1.00 more. Sam tells Sally that his produce company will not accept anything less than $1.00 more per bushel. Sally's Grocery Store contacts a produce company in a neighboring state and ends up buying potatoes at $0.75 a bushel more than what it had been paying Sam's Produce Company.

Does Sally's Grocery Store have a cause of action against Sam's Produce Company? If so, what is it? If you are advising Sally, what would you suggest the store do in this situation—and why?

Chapter 4
Arbitration and Mediation

Introduction

There are a number of legal methods and procedures available to businesses to resolve disputes that do not involve litigation. These alternative processes expedite the resolution of disputes without the expense of litigation. They are referred to as *alternative dispute resolution,* which is abbreviated as ADR.

Businesses often prefer ADR to formal litigation because with ADR, proprietary information, trade secrets, and other confidential information are not subject to intense scrutiny or disclosure as they may be in litigation. In litigation, the right of access to this information by the general public and news media can give competitors the opportunity to misappropriate and use the otherwise confidential information.

There are many types of formal arbitration. Each involves a process whereby the parties involved in the dispute agree to submit their arguments and evidence to a neutral person(s) for the purpose of adjudicating their claims. The evidentiary and procedural rules of arbitration are usually much less formal than they are in litigation, and there tends to be more flexibility in scheduling and the selection of the decisions makers. The most commonly used method of ADR is arbitration, which is where a neutral third party is selected by the parties involved in the dispute to hear the case and render an opinion. This opinion may or may not be binding on the parties, depending on the terms of the arbitration clause or agreement under which they are operating. In addition to arbitration, various forms of mediation, private judging, mini-trials, and moderated settlement conferences are available to companies who are unable to independently resolve their disputes but who wish to avoid the expense and time involved in the trial process. These are discussed in greater detail later in the chapter.

Each type of ADR offers certain advantages and disadvantages, which may make one process more appropriate for resolving a particular dispute than another. Therefore, the procedures, costs, and benefits of each ADR method should be carefully reviewed with legal counsel.

General Advantages of ADR

Some of the typical benefits a company may gain through ADR, as opposed to litigation, are as follows:

- *Disputes are resolved faster.* The reduction of delays in resolving legal claims was one of the driving forces behind the ADR movement. As the number of court cases continues to increase, the courts cannot expeditiously accommodate them. As a result, many parties find it more economical to obtain a final resolution of their disputes outside the courthouse.
- *There are significant cost savings.* In a recent study by the accounting firm of Deloitte Touche, 60 percent of all ADR users and 78 percent of those characterized as extensive users reported they had saved money by using ADR. Savings ranged from 11 percent to 50 percent of the cost of litigation. (Deloitte & Touche, Deloitte & Touche Litigation Services 1993 Survey of General and Outside Counsels: Alternative Dispute Resolution (ADR), Chicago: Deloitte & Touche, 1993, 16.)
- *Relationships are preserved.* ADR allows parties to resolve a dispute without the animosity that often destroys a business or personal relationship during litigation.
- *Confidential information is protected.* Litigation often results in the public disclosure of proprietary information, particularly in commercial disputes. Although one party may seek a protective order restricting the other party's access to its trade secrets, the mere process of obtaining such an order exposes the confidential information to outside scrutiny. ADR procedures allow the parties to resolve disputes while better protecting confidential information.
- *There is greater flexibility.* ADR allows the parties to tailor a dispute resolution process to the unique matter at hand. They can select the mechanism, determine the amount of information that needs to be exchanged, choose their own arbitrator or mediator, and agree on a format for the procedure.
- *The result is more durable.* Resolutions achieved by consensus of the disputants are less likely to be challenged than resolutions imposed by third parties.
- *There can be better, more creative solutions.* By giving litigants early and direct participation, ADR provides a greater opportunity for achieving a resolution based on the parties' real interests. Such agreements often produce a solution that makes more sense for the parties than one imposed by a court.

Situations in Which ADR Is Successful

ADR is mostly likely to be successful under these conditions:

- *An ADR contract clause is in place.* ADR is much more likely to be successful if there is an effective contract clause that provides for the use of ADR in the event of a future dispute.
- *There is a continuing relationship between the parties.* If a continuing relationship is possible (e.g., franchisors and franchisees), the chances of ADR success are increased. In these instances, the parties can then continue making money from each other for the duration of their agreement, rather than ending the relationship and suffering the cost and disruption of litigation.
- *The dispute is complex.* If a case involves highly complex technology, there is a significant chance that a jury and even a judge may become confused. Under these circumstances, ADR may be the best option, particularly if the proceedings are conducted before a neutral person who is an expert in the subject matter of the dispute. Since the parties themselves select the arbitrator, they have the opportunity to choose a well-qualified arbitrator rather than a randomly appointed judge or the uncertainties of the jury process.
- *Relatively little money is at stake.* If the amount of money in dispute is relatively small, the cost of litigation may approach or even exceed that amount.
- *Confidentiality is an important issue.* In an ADR proceeding, it is easier for the parties to maintain confidentiality, not just of their business information but also of the nature of the case. Sometimes the need for confidentiality is more important than any other consideration in selecting a dispute resolution process.

Situations Where ADR May Not Be Successful

In some instances ADR may not have a good chance of success:

- *The opposing party is skeptical and mistrusting.* The opposing party may see the other side's efforts to use ADR after a complaint has been filed as a way of getting an advantage in litigation. If the parties are extremely hostile to one another they may refuse to agree to otherwise well-qualified arbitrators simply because they were suggested by the opponent.
- *Parties or counsel have nasty attitudes.* When the parties or their counsel are extremely emotional, belligerent, or abusive, they are likely to be more concerned about airing their grievances than they are about resolving their dispute. This will obviously make it more difficult to successfully use non-binding ADR.
- *The case is one of many.* If the case at issue is one of many expected to be filed, it is not likely that the defendant will be motivated to agree to the use of ADR, particularly if it is non-binding. This may be one of those rare instances where litigation is actually more cost-effective due to the efficiency gained by the consolidation of multiple cases in a class action lawsuit.
- *Delays may benefit one party.* If a delay will benefit one of the parties, then the successful use of ADR will be diminished.
- *There are significant monetary imbalances.* If a significant monetary imbalance exists between parties and the wealthier party thinks it can wear down the other party through traditional litigation, then the wealthier party will likely refuse to agree to ADR.

Types of ADR

Arbitration

Arbitration may be a voluntary proceeding, such as when the parties to a contract have agreed to it as a means of dispute resolution, or it may be a compulsory, court-ordered procedure that is a prerequisite to actual litigation. Companies that wish to avoid the cost and delay of litigation should consider adding arbitration clauses to any contract prior to entering into it.

An arbitration clause should specify that the parties agree to submit any controversy or claim arising from the agreement or contract to binding (or non-binding) arbitration. It should also include the choice of location for the arbitration; the method for selecting the arbitrators who will hear the dispute; any limitations on the award that may be rendered by the arbitrator; which party will be responsible for the costs of the proceeding; whether the loser will pay the winner's attorneys' fees; and any special procedural rules that will govern the arbitration (i.e., those used by the American Arbitration Association).

The following arbitration clause is suggested for use by the American Arbitration Association (AAA):

> Any controversy or claim arising out of or relating to this contract, or the breach thereof, shall be settled by arbitration in accordance with the Commercial Arbitration Rules of the American Arbitration Association, and judgment rendered upon the award rendered by the arbitrator(s) may be entered in any court having jurisdiction thereof.

An important consideration for those drafting contracts is whether the decision of the arbitrator will be binding or non-binding. If the parties agree the award will be binding, then they must be prepared to live with the results.

Most often, the arbitrator selected is an attorney whose expertise may be negotiating rather than adjudicating, and therefore his or her decision often results in "splitting the baby down the middle," rather than a clear award for one party. Also, because no jury is involved, there is much less chance of recovering punitive or exemplary damages, since an attorney arbiter is much less likely to be swayed by emotional appeals.

As long as there is nothing unfair or illegal in the arbitration agreement or process, binding arbitration awards will usually be enforced by the court. However, the opinion rendered in a non-binding arbitration is advisory only. In non-binding arbitration, the parties may either accept the decision or reject it and proceed to litigation. One of the major criticisms of non-binding arbitration is that after the decision is rendered, the losing party often threatens to continue with litigation unless the monetary award is increased. As a result, the party that wins the arbitration is often coerced into paying or accepting less than the award recommended simply to avoid litigation after arbitration.

Sources of Arbitration Rules

There are many sources of arbitration rules. Unless the parties have drafted specific rules and procedures that will govern the arbitration, the two most commonly used are those created by the American Arbitration Association and the International Chamber of Commerce. Both can be obtained free of charge.

Hypothetical Case

Malcom Manufacturing Company is a growing business that makes and sells tires for off-road vehicles. Dune Buggy Inc. is Malcom's largest customer, with a contract to buy 1,000 tires per month for 24 months. Malcom uses chemicals it buys from China in the manufacturing of its tires. Recently, the news media have reported numerous accidents caused by tires made with these Chinese-supplied chemicals. So far, the tires with the problems have been those made by other manufacturers. Dune Buggy Inc. contacts Malcom Manufacturing and asks if its tires contain any of the Chinese-made chemical. When Malcom honestly answers that it does but that no problems have been reported with its tires, and that it is seeking another source for the chemical, Dune Buggy Inc. responds by saying it will not be accepting any more tires made by Malcom because they might be defective, and it can't risk putting them on their dune buggies. Dune Buggy does, in fact, refuse delivery of the next shipment of Malcom Manufacturing's tires and the fourteen months that remain on its contract. As a result, Malcom Manufacturing is forced to file for bankruptcy protection.

     If you are Malcom Manufacturing would you prefer to subject your breach of contract claims against Dune Buggy Inc. to ADR, or would you rather litigate them? What are the reasons for your decision? If you are Dune Buggy Inc., would you prefer to resolve Malcom's claim with ADR or through trial? What are the reasons for your decision?

Chapter 5
Business Ethics

Introduction

"If you have integrity, nothing else matters. If you don't have integrity, nothing else matters." *Alan K. Simpson, Senator, Wyoming*

What are business ethics? *Business ethics* are the ethical principles and problems that arise in a business environment.

It seems that the media are constantly bringing to light examples of excessive greed and malfeasance in the business community. Often, these situations result in the loss of public money, as well as confidence. As a result, the public is demanding more ethical behavior from both public and private businesses. Congress has responded by passing more and more stringent legislation in an effort to make companies behave in socially responsible and ethical ways.

Many corporate Web sites now contain a statement addressing their commitment to non-economic social values in addition to information promoting their products or services. Some corporations have defined their core values in the light of ethical considerations. An example would be paper product companies that emphasize their commitment to maintaining sustainable forests.

Of course, businesses exist to make money. There is nothing wrong or illegal about making a monetary profit from running a business. However, the manner in which some businesses conduct themselves disturbs some people and raises the question of ethical behavior. As we will see, good business ethics often makes good business sense.

In a research study conducted by the Institute of Business Ethics (IBE), it was found that companies that display a "clear commitment to ethical conduct" consistently outperform companies that do not display ethical conduct. (*Building the Business Case for Ethics*, Margolis, Walsh, Krehmeyer, Business Roundtable Institute for Corporate Ethics, 2006.)

Why Are Business Ethics Important?

If a company does not practice business ethics and breaks the law, it usually ends up being fined and sometimes prosecuted criminally. There are many examples of companies that have broken anti-trust, ethical, and environmental laws and received fines of millions of dollars. Yet these companies often continue such behavior because they believe the profit to be gained by these violations outweighs the fines they must pay. Billion-dollar profits make some companies ignore ethics, and they fail to see the other costs that result from their lack of ethics.

Even though a business makes millions of dollars, if the public sees it as exploiting child labor in a foreign country or needlessly destroying the environment during its manufacturing process, customers may shun its products and profits may suffer. The public's reaction to unethical businesses practices may prompt the company to adhere to proper business ethics. Many other companies pride themselves on their exemplary business ethics, without requiring the prod of public scorn.

Business ethics involves a lot more than compliance with laws, company policies, and financial regulations. Of course, the problems that result from these violations are the ones that are most likely to result in newspaper headlines when they are violated. Yet it's usually the less conspicuous things that cause businesses problems. Examples of areas where companies are often ethically challenged include deceptive pricing and promotion or advertising; selling unsafe or defective products; planned obsolescence; and poor service and high-pressure selling.

Because the ethical practices and social responsibility displayed by company managers is transmitted to employees it establishes the company's attitude, culture and ethical philosophy. This makes it extremely important that a company's ethical practices are displayed and enforced by top management.

Can a Business Be Both Ethical and Profitable?

According to the group Ethisphere, it is possible for a company to be both extremely ethical and extremely profitable. It has listed Alcoa, Kellogg's, John Deere, and General Electric as some of the most ethical corporations in the world. These are also some of the most profitable companies. (http://ethisphere.com/wme2008/)

A company's environmental policy, the way it treats its employees, and the communities in which it operates are all part of its overall behavior that determines how it is perceived by the public. A company's public perception affects it business relationships and its ability to recruit top talent.

When a person or business entity is considering investing in a particular company's stock, there are a number of things they look for. Aside from a company's profit margin, consideration is also given to the qualitative aspects of the company such as its public image and the products it sells. All of these things are taken into account when deciding whether to invest in the company. Therefore, a company that wants to encourage investment should have a strong sense of business ethics. An essential part of business ethics is a responsibility to the investor, http://www.articlesbase.com/business-articles/business-ethics-why-they-are-important-for-a-company-and-its-success-494408.html and companies that have a strong reputation for ethical business practices are also companies that tend to attract more investment from people who are new to the market.

In the business world, joint ventures are common. A business can be made or broken on just one joint venture, and part of the reason that joint ventures are successful is that they combine the forces of two extremely powerful companies on occasion.

When a company seeks a business partner, it usually looks for one that has a good reputation—both in terms of a track record and in terms of its overall business practices. One of the best ways to get a good reputation is to ensure that the company has a strong reputation for ethical business behavior.

Examples of Business Ethics

Business ethics can be examined from various perspectives. There is the perspective of the employee, the commercial enterprise, and society as a whole. Very often, situations arise in which there is conflict between one or more of the parties, so that serving the interest of one party is a detriment to the other(s). For example, a particular course of action might be good for the employee but it would be bad for the company or society.

There are many facets of business where ethics, or a lack thereof, are obvious. Here are examples of actions that raise questions of whether the behavior is ethical, to greater or lesser degrees:

Ethics of Production

- Using defective, addictive and inherently dangerous products and services (e.g., tobacco, alcohol, weapons, chemicals)
- Adversely affecting the environment: pollution, carbon emissions
- Using new technologies: genetically modified food, cell phone radiation
- Testing products on animals
- Using economically disadvantaged groups as test objects

Ethics of Intellectual Property, Knowledge, and Skills

- Engaging in patent, trademark, and copyright infringement
- Committing industrial espionage
- Raiding employees—the practice of attracting key employees away from a competitor to take unfair advantage of their knowledge or skills
- Employing all the most talented people in a specific field, regardless of need, in order to prevent any competitors employing them

International Commercial Ethics

- Taking advantage of international differences, such as outsourcing production and services to low-wage countries (e.g., clothing manufacturing and technical assistance service centers)
- Conducting international commerce with pariah states

Corporate Ethics Policies

Many companies have internal policies pertaining to the ethical conduct of employees as part of a comprehensive compliance and ethics program. These policies can be simple, very general policies, or they can be very detailed policies containing specific behavioral requirements. The latter are usually called *corporate ethics codes.*

Corporate ethics codes are generally meant to identify the company's expectations of employees and to offer guidance on how to handle some of the more common ethical problems that might arise in the course of doing business. Companies that have corporate ethics codes believe an ethics code will lead to greater ethical awareness, consistency in ethics application, and the avoidance of ethical disasters. Corporate ethics codes may also provide a defense to the company if it is sued for an ethics violation that is also a violation of law. For example, the company may be able to show that the conduct was that of a rogue employee who violated the company's ethics code and that the code demonstrates that the behavior is not sanctioned by the company or its management.

As part of its ethics policy and to aid interpretation and enforcement of its ethics code, companies may have an ethics officer called a compliance officer or business conduct officer.

Professional Codes of Ethics

Many professions, such as doctors, lawyers, and accountants, have an ethical code that members are expected to follow. If members violate these ethical codes, they may be required to appear before a professional disciplinary body, and their license may be suspended or revoked if the charges are proven.

Many businesses have their own ethical policies contained in a handbook or a separate *code of conduct*. Not only do these policies establish the company's ethical expectations and put employees on notice, but also they may serve as a defense to civil or criminal charges (e.g., sexual harassment).

Hypothetical Case

You work in the finance department of a large company. The company has a code of conduct that states, in part: "Employees are required to keep internal matters and disputes in strict confidence. Anyone caught speaking of internal business matters or disputes with non-employees shall be terminated from employment." A good friend is fired from his job in the company. He tells you he believes he was the victim of discrimination. A few days later you notice a notepad his boss left behind from a meeting. On it is written your friend's name, with a note next to it that says, "Next time, hire a female 22 to 32 years old." You tell your friend what you saw, and he wants you to talk to an EEOC investigator about it. Will you? Why or why not?

Chapter 6
Constitutional Law

Introduction

The U.S. legal system is based on common law, but unlike some common law countries, it also has a Constitution, which stands as the supreme law of the land. The body of law that deals with the interpretation of the U.S. Constitution is known as *constitutional law*.

Often, constitutional law deals with relationships between the states and the federal government, relationships between the states, and between the three branches of government. When these disputes arise, the final decision rests with the U.S. Supreme Court.

Supreme Court Justices

There are nine justices who serve on the U.S. Supreme Court. Each justice is nominated by the president, confirmed by the Senate, and serves for life (or until the justice retires).

The Senate confirmation process begins with hearings before the Senate Judiciary Committee and ends with a vote of the full Senate. A simple majority vote is required for confirmation.

Under the Constitution, justices who commit "high crimes or misdemeanors" are subject to impeachment and may be removed from office. There is no other mechanism for removing a justice from office.

Judicial Interpretation

The Supreme Court interprets the meaning of each clause of the Constitution. For example, the "full faith and credit clause" of the Constitution says that each state must recognize the public acts (laws), records, and judicial proceeding of the other states. It also guarantees that a citizen of one state is entitled to the "privileges and immunities" in every other state. For example, a divorce granted in one state must be recognized as valid in another state and its child support order enforced.

Interpreting the Constitution is often a difficult task. For example, marriages between same-sex couples are legally valid in Massachusetts (among other states). Do other states have to recognize them under the full faith and credit clause? Marriages in one state have always been recognized in all other states.

The answer, currently, is no: They don't have to recognize them. How can the legislature prevent gay "marriages" from being recognized under federal or given reciprocity? Congress passed the "Defense of Marriage Act" in 1996, which defines marriage as the union between one man and one woman. Thus, under federal law, there is no such thing as same-sex marriage. So by excluding same sex unions from the definition of marriage, it has eliminated the problem of enforcing same sex marriages.

According to the federal government, there are more than 1,138 rights and protections given to U.S. citizens upon marriage. These include Social Security benefits, veterans' benefits, health insurance, Medicaid, hospital visitation, estate taxes, retirement savings, pensions, family leave, and immigration law. However, many aspects of marriage law are determined by the states, not the federal government, and the Defense of Marriage Act does not prevent individual states from defining marriage as they see fit. Most legal scholars believe that the Constitution prohibits the federal government from imposing a definition of marriage onto the laws of the various states. As a result, there have been efforts to pass a Constitutional amendment that would prohibit same-sex marriage. In 2008, the California Supreme Court ruled that excluding same-sex couples from marriage is unconstitutional, effectively creating same-sex marriage in California. It cited an earlier decision (precedent) that reversed an interracial marriage ban. However, in response to this court decision, the voters of the state passed a state constitutional amendment prohibiting same-sex marriages that was upheld by California's Supreme Court. This is a legal issue on which the U.S. Supreme Court will likely be asked to render a decision.

Jurisprudence

The jurisprudence of Supreme Court Justices greatly influences their ruling on cases. *Jurisprudence* is commonly characterized as the study, knowledge, or science of law. In the United States, jurisprudence usually refers to the philosophy of law. Legal philosophy has many aspects, but the most common seeks to analyze, explain, classify, and criticize entire bodies of law. Legal treatises and law school textbooks represent this type of scholarship. The second type of jurisprudence compares and contrasts law with other fields of knowledge such as economics, religion, and the social sciences. There is a third type of jurisprudence that seeks to reveal the historical, moral, and cultural basis of a specific legal concept. This form of jurisprudence focuses on finding the answer to more abstract questions such as, "What is the purpose of law?"

Not only are there different types of jurisprudence, but also there are different philosophies of jurisprudence. Formalism, or conceptualism, treats law like math or science. Formalists believe that a judge identifies the relevant legal principles, applies them to the facts of a case, and logically deduces a rule that will govern the outcome of the dispute. In contrast, proponents of legal realism believe that most cases present tough questions that judges must resolve by balancing the interests of all the parties and creating a ruling that sides with one party in the dispute. This rule is based in part on the political, economic, and psychological inclinations of the judge. Some legal realists even believe that a judge is able to shape the outcome of the case based on personal biases.

Apart from the realist–formalist difference, there is the classic debate over the appropriate sources of law between positivist and natural law schools of thought. *Positivists* argue that there is no connection between law and morality and the only sources of law are rules that have been expressly enacted by governments or courts of law. *Naturalists* insist that the rules enacted by government are not the only source of law. They argue that moral philosophy, religion, human reason, and individual conscience are also integral parts of the law.

Sometimes the differences between the schools of jurisprudence are not that easy to distinguish. The legal philosophy of a particular legal scholar or justice may contain a combination of beliefs from more than one school of legal thought.

How Cases Make Their Way to the Supreme Court

Cases make their way to the Supreme Court in one of two ways. Most cases begin in a state court. Usually, they start in a city or county court and then progress until they reach the state's highest court. From there, if it involves a federal issue, the case can be appealed directly to the U.S. Supreme Court. Cases involving the application or interpretation of federal law begin in federal district court and move through the Court of Appeals (circuit court) and then to the U.S. Supreme Court.

Interpreting Constitutional Clauses

Unlike trial courts, the U.S. Supreme Court is not concerned with the guilt or innocence of those accused and convicted of crimes. Its purpose and sole responsibility is to make sure that laws are passed and administered in ways that the U.S. Constitution allows. This means that the Court only hears cases where the parties are arguing about constitutional issues. For example, imagine that the Court hears the case of *State v. Defendant* in which Defendant was convicted of downloading pornography in violation of state law. The U.S. Supreme Court will not consider whether Defendant is guilty or innocent of the crime. Rather, it will consider only whether the law itself conforms to requirements of the Constitution or whether the process used to convict Defendant meets constitutional requirements. This distinction is important because people often see an injustice that seems to have been done to a defendant and expect an appellate court to give justice to the wronged party, but this does not always happen. Often, appellate courts cannot administer justice to individuals because their sole responsibility is to interpret the Constitution and the constitutionality of federal and state laws.

The Due Process Clause

The *due process clause* of the Fourteenth Amendment has been interpreted by the Supreme Court as affording citizens protection from interference by the state when exercising their rights listed in the first eight amendments. The Fourteenth Amendment also guarantees the equal protection of the laws. This Constitutional amendment requires that the laws of a state must treat a person in the same manner as others in similar conditions and circumstances. For example, when the Fourteenth Amendment of the Constitution promises "life, liberty," and "equal protection of the laws" to "any person," it is referring to acts that the government must *refrain* from doing, not to any positive duty the government has to act. A violation of the due process clause would occur, for example, if a state prohibited an individual from entering into an employment contract because he or she was a member of a particular race—for example, "Only white males can be employed by the United States government." The only time the government has a positive duty to act is when it has already wrongfully deprived a person of liberty.

Since the 1940s, courts have increasingly read positive rights into the Constitution, which according to some has deprived citizens of negative rights to which they are entitled.

Civil Liberties

The Constitution also guarantees to the people certain civil liberties such as the right to be free of government interference, and civil rights such as the right to be treated as a free and equal citizen of the country. These liberties and rights are spelled out in the Bill of Rights, which is the first ten amendments to the Constitution. Additional civil liberties such as the freedom of speech, press, and religion are also part of the Bill of Rights.

Checks and Balances

By dividing and limiting various governmental powers, the Constitution creates a system of checks and balances. If one branch of government threatens to become too powerful, other branches may act to block or thwart it. For example, if the president steps beyond his powers, Congress can refuse to provide funds or the courts can rule the president's actions unconstitutional. An example occurred when President Nixon attempted to claim executive privilege to keep Congress from examining audiotapes it had subpoenaed, which were in his possession. The Supreme Court ruled that the Executive (president) did not have the authority to ignore or nullify the legitimate exercise of Congressional powers.

Necessary and Proper Clause

The Constitution also grants Congress the right to make laws that it deems "necessary and proper" to carry out its enumerated powers. This implied power gives Congress wide leeway in lawmaking.

The Commerce Clause

The commerce clause of the Constitution gives Congress the authority to create regulatory agencies that, for example, set railroad rates, regulate the quality of foods and drugs, and subject more and more of the economy to governmental oversight.

Specifically, the commerce clause states that Congress has the power to regulate commerce with foreign nations, and among the several states, and with the Indian tribes.

The Supreme Court's interpretation of the commerce clause has changed over time. How the Constitution's drafters understood the word *commerce* is a subject of disagreement among scholars. In the late nineteenth century, the Supreme Court employed a narrow definition of the commerce clause, pointing to the Tenth Amendment of the Constitution, which reserves power to the states that are not delegated to the federal government. Because of its narrow interpretation, it ruled that activities such as manufacturing were not part of interstate commerce, finding instead that they were purely local activities. As local activities, only the states would be allowed to regulate them. The Court struck down several congressional attempts to regulate labor practices, wages, and industrial conditions as a result. But in the late 1930s, in the midst of the Great Depression, the Supreme Court began to change its interpretation. By 1940, after President Franklin Roosevelt appointed several new justices, the Court's position evolved to the point that it concluded that anything that affects interstate commerce falls within Congress's commerce power. This interpretation, combined with the "necessary and proper" authority granted under the Constitution, has been used to justify all sorts of government regulation of business activities.

Since the interpretation of the commerce clause in the 1940s, Congress has had a free hand to regulate industrial and economic activities in many ways. Major civil rights laws outlawing discrimination, for example, were enacted under the commerce power.

Preemption

Under the U.S. Constitution's supremacy clause, if state laws conflict with federal objectives, then the federal programs trump and "preempt" the conflicting state provisions. In some instances, federal law will preempt an entire field. When the Constitution or federal statute gives the federal government sole control over an area, it *preempts* the states from passing any law in that area. For example, if the federal government were to enact a law that says, "No state shall pass any law that regulates or attempts to regulate the discharge of chemicals into public waterways," and a state passed a law that said its coal plants could discharge effluents into state rivers, its law would be declared void and unenforceable because the federal law preempted it.

If the federal government passes a law that regulates a field that the U.S. Constitution says is reserved to the states, then the U.S. Supreme Court may declare the federal law unconstitutional. For example, Article V of the Constitution gives the states the power "to require Congress to convene a constitutional convention for the purpose of proposing amendments to or revising the terms of the Constitution" so if Congress attempted to pass a law saying the Senate could convene a constitutional convention for this purpose it would be struck down as an unconstitutional attempt to pre-empt state authority.

Hypothetical Case

The state of Magnanimous passes a law taxing all Internet sales to its residents. Two years later, Congress passes a law taxing all Internet sales at a 2 percent rate. Has the tax law passed by Magnanimous been preempted? Why or why not?

Chapter 7
Statutory Law

Introduction

Statutory law is distinguished from constitutional law and common law in that it is the body of law enacted by a legislature. Both the U.S. Congress and state legislatures enact statutes either by bill or by joint resolution. These *statutes* are laws. According to the constitution, federal statutes have superiority over state statutes, and state statutes are superior to the common law and municipal statutes (ordinances).

How Statutory Law Differs from Common Law

Statutory law differs from common law in that common law refers to law developed through court cases (precedent) rather than through legislatively enacted statutes.

Statutory law is written law that is drafted and passed by a legislature or other governing body. It clarifies the functioning of government, regulates civil order, defines criminal conduct, and codifies existing law. In addition to the statutes passed by the national or state legislature, municipalities may also pass their own administrative regulations and statutes, which are called ordinances and have the force of law. Although ordinances are subordinate to the law of state or nation, they are still a part of the body of statutory law.

Statutory law is inferior to constitutional law, and courts exercise the power of judicial review when they declare statutes unconstitutional. By declaring a statute unconstitutional, a court is saying that the law violates constitutional requirements and is therefore invalid.

Statutory law is codified under titles describing the areas of action to which they pertain, and these titles are grouped together in codes. The administrative branch of government often enforces statutory law through administrative rules and regulations that have the effect of law as long as they conform to the limits set by the statutes that created them.

Depending on the subject, state law or federal law may be controlling. For example, corporate law and wills and probate administration are two areas governed by state statutes, while patent and laws are governed by federal statutes. Consumer law is covered by both state and federal statutes, while protecting consumers from deceptive trade practices and unsafe products and activities that threaten a consumer are mostly governed by state laws.

Employment law is typically governed by federal statutes, while each state has its own statutes that govern certain areas of employment that have not been preempted by federal law. Antitrust laws are also federal statutes, even though some states also have their own laws that deal with this subject.

Statutory law is sometimes created as a response to a specific situation or circumstance. The legislature may decide that certain business practices need to be regulated. For example, the Environmental Protection Agency is an agency that has statutes and regulations to protect the public and enforce laws. By codifying environmental laws in this manner, the government provides uniformity in what all states must do rather than the differences that can result when relying on varying case law.

A court's interpretation of a statute may also become a precedent that lower courts must follow in subsequent decisions. In this way, statutory law and common law become one, since courts must interpret and apply statutory law. Since common law can be ambiguous, statutory law provides a solid framework around which common law can be built. It is the interpretation of these laws by courts that forms the basis of common law.

Chapter 8
Administrative Law

Introduction

What is administrative law? Administrative law is a branch of public law, often referred to as *regulatory law*. As a body of law, administrative law deals with the decision making of administrative tribunals, boards, or commissions of government agencies. These administrative agencies are part of a national regulatory scheme that deals with international trade, manufacturing, taxation, the environment, and transportation. Administrative law consists of laws and legal principles governing the administration and regulation of both federal and state government agencies. Such agencies are delegated power by Congress (or in the case of a state agency, the state legislature) to act as agents for the executive branch of government. Most often, administrative agencies are organized under the executive branch of government and are created to protect a public interest rather than to vindicate private rights.

Examples of administrative agencies are the Environmental Protection Agency (which was established to protect environmental resources) and those governing taxation, immigration, and the regulation of public utilities. Taxation disputes are the most commonly contested administrative decisions. Most government agencies have the authority to make rules, enforce those rules, and contain a procedure to adjudicate the legality of its actions and decisions.

How Administrative Law Works

U.S. federal agencies have the power to adjudicate, legislate, and enforce laws within their specific areas of delegated power. Agencies have the power to "legislate" by enacting regulations through rule making. These ruled are contained and codified in the Code of Federal Regulations (CFR).

The authority of all administrative agencies comes from statutes, which must comply with constitutional constraints. Agencies do not have the power to enact a regulation if the regulation is an unconstitutional delegation of power or the statute that created it explicitly denies it such authority. Regulations will also be struck down if Congress has enacted a separate regulatory scheme for the agency or the regulation does not serve the "public convenience, interest, or necessity." Also, if the regulation is outside the agency's statutory purpose, the court may declare it is invalid.

Each agency is responsible for a particular body of substantive law, such as taxation or professional licensing, but certain procedural principles apply to all agencies. If an agency does not have its own procedural rule, it will follow those established in the Administrative Procedures Act.

An administrative law judge (ALJ) is the official who presides over an *administrative hearing,* which is like a trial, to resolve disputes between a government agency and someone affected by a decision of that agency.

Rule Making and Adjudication

Agency acts are divided into two broad categories: rule making and adjudication. Generally, an act is adjudicative in nature if all of the following are true:

- It involves a small number of people.
- The individuals involved are uniquely affected by the act.
- The decision is based on the facts of an individual case rather than policy concerns.

The adjudicative process is used to resolve disputes between the agency and those affected by its decisions. This process may rely on hearings conducted before administrative law judges, or a panel of judges, or an official's review of written records. The final decision of an agency's adjudicative body may be appealed to a court.

The Administrative Procedure Act

The Administrative Procedures Act states that *rulemaking* is "an agency process for formulating, amending, or repealing a rule." A *rule,* in turn, is "the whole or a part of an agency statement of general or particular applicability and future effect designed to implement, interpret, or prescribe law or policy." *Adjudication* is "an agency process for the formulation of an order," and an *order* is "the whole or part of a final disposition . . . of an agency in a matter other than rule making but including licensing."

Judicial Review of Administrative Agencies

Judicial review is the power of the courts to nullify the acts of the executive and/or the legislative branches of government when it finds them to have violated the law. Judicial review is an example of the "separation of powers" doctrine whereby the judicial branch reviews the actions of the other two branches of government. Courts have the power to decide all relevant questions of law, interpret constitutional and statutory provisions, and determine the meaning or applicability of an agency's action and regulations. Generally, however, courts will not review an administrative decision until the agency itself has completed its own review and rendered a final decision on it. Before a court will hear a case that comes from an administrative agency, it determines if the case is "ripe" and ready for its review. If a final decision on the case has not been rendered by the administrative agency or by a tribunal or other adjudicative body, it will not hear the case.

When courts do review the decision of an administrative agency, they usually give wide discretion to the agency and are reluctant to overturn its decision. They tend to believe the administrative agency is a specialist in the subject it governs and will reverse an agency's decision only if one the following is true:

- The evidence seriously contradicts the agency's conclusion.
- Ex parte contact has tainted the agency's decision.
- Relevant and contradictory points of view were not considered by the agency.
- A significant change in the agency's policy was not fully explained.

When reviewing an administrative agency's actions, the courts examine the authority given the agency by the statute that created it, known as the *enabling act*. Congress often specifies the terms of judicial review on the merits in the enabling act. Typically, an enabling act will allow the court to reverse an administrative tribunal's decision if it determines that the decision is not supported by substantial evidence or it is arbitrary and capricious. This is a difficult burden to meet, however, since the courts will usually uphold an agency's decision as long as it can find a rational basis to do so.

Hypothetical Case

You work for Sam's Manufacturing Company, which makes speedboats. The Environmental Protection Agency (EPA) has charged the company with polluting a lake near its manufacturing plant and test facility. The complaint filed by the EPA alleges that the company has discharged large amounts of gasoline into the lake during its constant testing of boat engines. According to the EPA, the company's engine-testing process violates an EPA regulation, which limits the acceptable amount of gasoline that can be discharged into lakes and streams. A hearing was conducted before the EPA and the company's attorney presented evidence that it tested sixty boats per month in the lake for ten minutes each. The company argued that this produced less pollution than the boats used by the boats owned and operated by people who lived on the lake. The administrative law judge ruled against the company. Afterward, you learn that the administrative law judge has a sister who lives on the lake and has complained about all the noise caused by Sam's product testing. If the company appeals the EPA's decision what will your arguments be in support of the company? What will they be in support of the EPA's decision?

Chapter 9
Intentional Torts

Introduction

What is a tort? A tort is a violation of a duty imposed by civil law, which causes injury to a person or property. There are three types of torts: intentional torts, negligence torts, and strict liability torts.

Intentional Torts

Intentional torts are caused by a deliberate (intentional) act, and the result is foreseeable. For example, if a person picks up a baseball bat and swings it at another person, the act is intentional, and it is foreseeable that it will injure the other person. The act of intentionally touching another person without permission and with the intent to cause injury is a battery. Other examples of intentional torts are defamation, fraud, and intentional infliction of emotional distress.

To be responsible for the commission of an intentional tort, a person must have intended the consequences of an act, or the person must believe the consequences of it are substantially certain to result. Furthermore, if the intent to injure someone is shown, it doesn't matter that the intended victim was not the one actually injured. The intent to commit a tort can be transferred between victims. Thus, if Kristen throws a rock intending to hit William and he ducks with the result that the rock hits Susie, who was standing behind William, Kristen can be charged with battery against Susie even though she didn't intend to injure Susie.

Intentional Business Torts

In the business setting, an intentional business tort is an action a party undertakes with the desire to interfere with another's business relationship or business expectancy and the action is substantially certain to result in such interference (i.e., it is foreseeable). For any tort to be actionable in court, the interference must result in some form of demonstrable damage or injury.

Examples of intentional business torts are:

- Defamation
- Fraudulent misrepresentation
- Unfair competition
- Interference with a business relationship (contract or expectancy)

Defamation

To be successful in any court case, a party has to prove all of the elements of the offense that the law requires. If a plaintiff fails to prove any element of an offense, then the judge or jury must find the defendant not guilty in a criminal case or not responsible in a civil case. The elements that must be demonstrated may be specified in a statute or derived from common law. Defamation is an offense most often associated with individuals, such as when one person wrongfully accuses another person of being a thief or a liar. However, defamation can also occur in the business setting where one corporation, or an individual, tells people a particular corporation is polluting a river or cheating its customers and that information is false. Although the elements of defamation may differ, depending on state statute or jurisdictional precedent, they usually consist of all of the following:

- The statement is false, and the defendant knew it was false when the statement was made.
- The statement is communicated to a third party.
- The statement causes injury.

Defamation may occur in either of two forms: *libel,* which is defamation in a written form and *slander,* which is defamation in a verbal form.

Corporations have protectable business reputations based on their corporate competence, integrity, and solvency. For example, the Home Shopping Network (HSN) claimed in public statements that it suffered millions of dollars in losses because GTE provided it with defective telephone equipment and services. HSN sued GTE because of this allegation, and GTE responded with a counterclaim for defamation. GTE claimed HSN's public statements about the telephone equipment and services it provided were false. The jury agreed with GTE's position and awarded the company $100 million in damages. (*Zimmerman v. Home Shopping Network, Inc.* 1989 WL 102488 (Del.Ch.), 15 Del. J. Corp. L. 1185)

In another case, *Brown & Williamson Tobacco Corp. v. Jacobson* (1987), Brown & Williamson sued a television anchorman who stated that Brown & Williamson had adopted an advertising strategy deliberately designed to induce minors to begin smoking cigarettes.

Reporting erroneous and damaging credit information about a company can also result in a defamation lawsuit. When Dun & Bradstreet falsely reported that Greenmoss Builders, Inc. had filed for bankruptcy, it was forced to respond to a defamation lawsuit. In recent years, companies appear to be more willing to pursue claims for harm to their reputations instead of simply tolerating false statements about them as part of doing business.

Defenses to Defamation

There are several defenses that may be used to successfully defend against a defamation claim:

- The information is true.
- The information is opinion.
- The information is satire.
- No reasonable person would believe it.

Defamation against Public Officials and Celebrities

Public officials and public personalities have less protection from defamation than average citizens. This is because the law assumes that a person who seeks public office or fame must accept a certain amount of "gossip" or talk about them as a result as a natural consequence of their notoriety. As a result, for a claim of defamation to be successful against public figures, the public figure must show also show the additional element of actual malice, meaning the statement was made knowing it was false or with reckless disregard of the truth.

Fraudulent Misrepresentation

Fraud consists of injuring another person by deliberately deceiving them. For example, if a business submits materially misleading financial statements to a bank in an attempt to secure a loan and the bank, relying on the statements, lends money to the business, the bank will have a fraud claim against the business if it later defaults on the loan.

A fraud claim may not only result from an affirmative statement that is untrue, but also from the failure to disclose a material fact if a defendant owed a duty to speak the truth and disclose information. For example, if a real estate agent represents both a buyer and seller of real property, he or she may be liable for fraud if the advisor knows that the property contains toxic chemicals and fails to tell the buyer.

There are six elements of fraudulent misrepresentation:

1. *The statement is false.* This is known as a false representation or false statement.
2. *The false statement (misrepresentation) is material to the transaction.* This means it an essential part of the transaction at hand. For example, if you are selling a washing machine and you lie about having a new Corvette, it may be fraudulent misrepresentation but it is not material to this transaction.
3. *The misrepresentation is made with knowledge that is false, or with reckless disregard as to whether or not it is true.* This means that either a party knows the information is a lie or it has no reason to believe the statement is true. For example, if you are selling an old painting you found in the attic and you tell prospective purchasers it was painted by Monet in an effort to induce them to buy it, it is possible that it is true, but it is extremely unlikely to be true.
4. *The misrepresentation is made with the intention of inducing the other party to act or to refrain from acting.* This occurs when a party intentionally tries to affect the behavior of the other party in a transaction with a lie, such as falsely telling a prospective purchaser the car was previously owned by Elvis Presley.
5. *The other party has to rely on the lie.* A party must rely on the misrepresentation in order to have a viable cause of action. For example, a buyer cannot sue the seller for lying about Elvis Presley being the former owner of the car if he doesn't buy the car.
6. *The lie must cause the other party to suffer damages.* This means the plaintiff must suffer actual harm by the transaction. For example, if the seller lies and says the ring contains a fake diamond when it actually contains a real diamond, the buyer has suffered no injury and has no basis (or reason) to sue.

Unfair Competition

The law of unfair competition comprises all torts that cause an economic injury to a business through deceptive or wrongful business practices. Unfair competition consists of two broad categories. First, the term *unfair competition* includes those torts that are meant to confuse consumers concerning the source of a product. An example of this practice would be the labeling of an inferior product so that it looks like a much more expensive competitor. The other category, *unfair trade practices,* comprises all other forms of unfair competition.

What constitutes an "unfair" act or practice varies with the context of the business, the action being examined, and the facts of each case. The most familiar example of unfair competition is *trademark infringement*. Another common form of unfair competition is *misappropriation*. Misappropriation involves the unauthorized use of intangible assets that are not protected by trademark or copyright laws. Other practices that are included in unfair competition include false advertising, "bait and switch" selling tactics, unauthorized substitution of one brand of goods for another, theft of trade secrets, breach of a restrictive covenant, use of confidential information by former employees to solicit customers, and false representation of products or services.

The law of unfair competition is mainly governed by state law. However, in the areas of trademark, copyright, and false advertising, federal law usually applies.

Part of the Federal Trade Commission's (FTC) responsibility is to protect consumers from deceptive trade practices. The FTC indirectly protects competitors because some deceptive trade practices, such as bait-and-switch tactics that injure consumers, also injure competing businesses. Some states have enacted their own laws dealing with specific types of unfair competition. Remember, if there is a conflict between federal and state law, the state law will be preempted.

Remedies for unfair competition may include getting the party at fault to pay monetary damages for their false representations; refunding any revenue lost as a result of the unfair business practice; a cessation of the unfair acts, or the payment of a large fine, along with other government sanctioned penalties.

Intentional Interference with a Business Contract or Relationship

The tort of interference with contractual relations permits a plaintiff to recover damages based on a claim that the defendant interfered with the plaintiff's contractual or other business relations. To be successful, the lack of justification in procuring the breach of contract or interference in the relationship requires a plaintiff to prove that the defendant's interference with the contract was improper. If a defendant's interference with a business relationship or a contract is justified, then such action is not actionable. Only improper interference is actionable.

Elements of intentional interference with a business contract are as follows:

- There is a contract or other economic relationship between the plaintiff and some third party with the possibility of future economic benefit to the plaintiff.
- The defendant knew of the contract or relationship.
- The defendant perpetrated intentional acts with the desire to disrupt the relationship.
- The defendant's actions actually disrupt the relationship.
- The plaintiff suffers damages proximately caused by the acts of the defendant.

There is an important limitation to the use of this tort as a remedy for the disruption of contractual relationships. It can only be asserted against a third party. Courts typically base this on the underlying policy of protecting the expectations of contracting parties from interference by outsiders who have no legitimate social or economic interest in the contractual relationship. Therefore, it limits the tort of interference with a contract to those who are not a party to the contract.

There is a threshold causation requirement to establish the tort of intentional interference with prospective economic advantage. What is required is proof that it is reasonably probable that the lost economic advantage would have been realized *but for* the defendant's interference.

In determining whether a defendant's interference in a business relationship is improper, courts may consider seven things:

1. The nature of the defendant's conduct
2. The defendant's motive

3. The interests of the plaintiff with which the defendant's conduct interferes
4. The interests sought to be advanced by the defendant
5. The social interests in protecting the freedom of action of the defendant and the contractual interests of the plaintiff
6. The proximity or remoteness of the defendant's conduct to the interference
7. The relations between the parties

Hypothetical Case

You start a new company that produces automobiles that run on natural gas. The company does much better than expected and takes a large market share away from traditional auto companies. However, when you go to pick up your largest order ever for natural gas (NG) widgets, the supplier tells you it can't (or won't) sell them to you. Your investigation reveals that Toyota has paid the supplier $3 million for its promise not to supply you with NG widgets. Can you sue Toyota for intentional interference with a business relationship? Why or why not, and what must you prove to be successful?

Hypothetical Case

You start a new company that produces a Web browser that directly competes with Microsoft's Internet Explorer. Several trade magazines tout the superiority of your browser, and sales really go up. However, just when things are taking off and you think you can pay off your business loan, sales plummet. You're at a loss to figure out why, until a customer asks why your company owns a subsidiary that hunts baby seals and clubs them to death to sell the fur to Japanese clothiers. When you get done uttering your expletives, you ask where the customer got such an outrageous idea. The customer says it was posted on a chat board for software developers by someone who claimed to work for your company. You take a look and verify that such a posting exists. Of course, you submit a posting that refutes the lie, but sales don't come back up. What, if any, legal cause of action do you have? What can you do if your corporate "detectives" trace the false posting to an employee of Microsoft?

Chapter 10
Negligence

Introduction

What is negligence? Legally actionable *negligence* is doing something that a reasonably prudent person would not do, or the failure to do something that a reasonably prudent person would do under like circumstances. In negligence cases, the perpetrator doesn't intend the consequences of his act to harm anyone, but they do.

The negligence concept is centered on the principle that every individual should exercise a minimum degree of care so as not to cause harm to others. To determine negligence, the court looks at whether a person of ordinary prudence, in the same situation and possessing the same knowledge, would have anticipated (foreseen) that someone might be injured by his or her action (or inaction).

Elements of Negligence

In most jurisdictions, to win a negligence case a plaintiff must prove five elements:

1. The defendant owed the plaintiff a duty of care.
2. The defendant breached that duty.
3. The defendant's conduct caused the plaintiff injury.
4. The injury/harm was foreseeable.
5. The plaintiff actually suffered an injury.

Duty of Care

If the law imposes a *duty of care,* a defendant breaches this duty by failing to behave the way a "reasonable" person would behave in similar circumstances. A reasonable person is a person in the same occupation or situation as that of the plaintiff or person being examined.

In addition, a successful plaintiff must demonstrate that the defendant's failure to uphold his duty is the reason he suffered injury. There must be a factual connection between the actions (or inaction) of the defendant and the injury suffered by the plaintiff. Finally, the type of harm caused must be foreseeable.

Generally, if the defendant can foresee injury to a particular person, than he has a duty of care to him. Courts will look to see if there was conduct that violates a duty of care owed someone, whether that conduct was the cause of the plaintiff's injury and whether, in fact, the plaintiff did suffer injury or damages.

Here are two examples of a breached duty of care resulting in a negligence claim:

1. A shopping mall owner breaches its duty to provide a safe place for shoppers by not fixing a faulty automatic door and a person is injured when the door closes too quickly.
2. A doctor breaches her duty to provide competent medical treatment by amputating the wrong leg of a patient, thus causing an additional operation and loss of mobility.

Reasonable Person

When determining whether a duty has been breached, the law employs the hypothetical reasonable person. This reasonable person is used to determine if the defendant acted responsibly or negligently under the circumstances. A person acts negligently if he or she departs from the conduct expected of a reasonably prudent person acting under similar circumstances. The hypothetical reasonable person provides an objective by which the conduct of others is judged. In law, the reasonable person is not an average person or a typical person but a composite of the community's judgment as to how the typical community member should behave in situations that pose a threat of harm to the public. Even though the majority of people in the community may behave in a certain way, that behavior does not establish the standard of conduct of the reasonable person. For example, a majority of people in a community might run red lights, but running red lights might still fall below the community's standards of safe conduct.

Causation

To determine whether a result was foreseeable, the court examines how remote the cause was. There are two types of causation under the law:

1. Cause-in-fact
2. Proximate (or legal) cause

Cause-in-Fact: The "But-For" Test

Cause-in-fact is determined by the *but-for test*. This test asks: But for the defendant's action, would the result have happened? For example, but for defendant's conduct in running the red light, would the collision have happened?

Proximate Cause

Proximate cause is an event sufficiently related to be recognized as a cause of the injury. It is the initial act that sets off a natural and continuous sequence of events that produces injury.

For example, if you roll a ball down the hill, a stranger picks it up and throws it through a window, the window breaks, and the broken glass hits a person who was sitting next to the window and cuts her arm, what is the proximate cause of the injured arm?

Most courts would conclude that the intervening act of the stranger picking up the ball and throwing it through the window is the proximate cause of the injury, not your act of rolling the ball down the hill. It is not the "but for you rolling the ball down the hill" that is controlling but the "but for the stranger picking up the ball and throwing it through the window" that is the operable issue.

Therefore, if an intervening act interrupts the natural chain of events and causes an accident and injury, the person who set the initial events in motion will not be found negligent.

In some jurisdictions, it may be sufficient for the plaintiff to show that the defendant's breach of duty made the risk of injury more probable. An example of this would be if a mechanic failed to inspect a vehicle's tires as required and the worn tires caused the car to skid during rain so it crossed the centerline and hit another car. The mechanic's failure to inspect the tires as required greatly increased the risk of this foreseeable accident.

Damages

In negligence cases, the injury suffered must be actual, not merely speculative. That means a negligence case claiming, "I would have been a professional skater if you hadn't broken my ankle," will not be successful in recovering lost money for the lost income of a professional skater. However, if a person *is* a professional skater and can prove how much money he makes in that capacity, he may be successful in recovering his lost income if someone breaks his ankle.

Damages in negligence cases are usually compensatory. Usually, money is awarded to compensate a person for the injury suffered. This means money may be awarded for loss of income, reimbursement for costs incurred because of the negligent act, or medical expenses. Some states allow punitive damages, which can be large so as to serve as a deterrent to others who might otherwise be tempted to engage in the same type of behavior (e.g., manufacturers of dangerous products).

Defenses to Negligence

As with all causes of action, the law recognizes certain defenses that will exculpate the defendant. In negligence cases, there are three main defenses:

1. Assumption of the risk
2. Contributory negligence
3. Comparative negligence

Assumption of the Risk

Assumption of the risk is where a person voluntarily engages in an activity when there is an obvious risk of injury. Some activities where an individual is assumed to have accepted a risk of injury are skiing, hang gliding, and horseback riding.

Contributory Negligence

If plaintiffs, through their own negligence, contributed to causing the injury they suffered as a result of defendant's negligence, the court may preclude any recovery from the defendant. For example, if a pedestrian crosses a road at a place other than a designated crosswalk and isn't paying attention and is hit by a driver who is also driving carelessly, the pedestrian has contributed to her own injury.

At common law, contributory negligence was an absolute defense to a negligence claim. If a defendant successfully raised the contributory negligence defense and was able to prove that the plaintiff was even 1% at fault for their injuries, the defendant would be able to avoid any liability for negligence. This often led to an injustice where the negligence of a plaintiff or claimant was slight in comparison with that of the defendant. As a result, most jurisdictions in the United States have modified this doctrine, either by court decision or by legislation, and have changed the name to comparative negligence.

Comparative Negligence

Comparative negligence was developed as a fairer way of dealing with the situation of plaintiffs contributing to their own injuries by modifying the "all or nothing" result of contributory negligence. In comparative negligence, rather than awarding no damages at all to a plaintiff who is partially responsible for their own injury, the jury reduces the compensation awarded by a percentage that reflects the degree to which the plaintiff's negligence contributed to them. For example, if the jury determines that the plaintiff is 30 percent at fault for the injuries received because she failed to cross the street at the crosswalk, the plaintiff's recovery will be reduced by that amount and she will recover for the 70 percent of the injuries attributable to the careless driver.

Minors

A minor (person under seventeen years of age) is not held to the same standard of care as an adult. A minor is required to exercise the degree of care that ordinarily is exercised by minors of like maturity, intelligence, and capacity under similar circumstances.

Hypothetical Case

Sarah Storekeeper runs a boutique business selling handmade soaps and candles. She often makes the products at a work area in the store so customers can watch. This was a very good way of attracting people into the store. One day, a woman and her five-year-old child were watching Sarah make candles and the woman and Sarah became engaged in a discussion about the difference in candle-making techniques. Neither one of them noticed as the five-year-old grabbed the container of melted wax, tipping it over and spilling its contents on his face and neck. The child's mother filed a lawsuit on behalf of her son, claiming Sarah's negligence resulted in $100,000 of medical bills and permanent scarring and disfigurement to the child. What are the arguments on behalf of the mother that support the claim of negligence against Sarah? What arguments may Sarah raise in defense?

Chapter 11
Strict Liability

Introduction

What is strict liability? *Strict liability* is liability imposed by law in instances where an activity is so dangerous that the law imposes a special burden on anyone who engages in it. Fault is not an issue in strict liability cases.

The rationale behind the development of strict liability is that if the harm results from an activity that, though lawful, is unusual, extraordinary, exceptional, or inappropriate under the circumstances, the perpetrator should be held accountable regardless of whether or not they acted negligently. Common hazardous activities that could result in strict liability include storing explosives or flammable liquids, blasting, accumulating sewage, and emitting toxic fumes. Although these activities may be appropriate or normal in one location, they may not be in another. For example, storing explosives in quantity will create an unusual and unacceptable risk in the midst of a large city but not in a remote area. If an explosion occurs in the remote area, strict liability will be imposed only if the explosives were stored in an unusual or abnormal way.

Strict liability is sometimes called absolute liability. It is the theory that holds an individual or corporation legally responsible for damages or injury even if they were not at fault or negligent. Strict liability has been applied to hold an employer absolutely liable for the torts of its employees, but today it is most commonly used when dealing with defectively manufactured products. In addition, public policy practices require that certain activities may only be conducted if the person conducting them is willing to insure others against the harm that could result from the risks the dangerous activity creates.

Strict liability does not apply in situations where the individual has willingly assumed the risk of injury, such as sky diving or other dangerous sports. It is only applicable when liability has been imposed by law, i.e. by a statute.

Strict Liability in Product Liability

In product liability cases involving injuries caused by manufactured goods, strict liability has had a major impact on litigation since the 1960s. In 1963, the California Supreme Court became the first court to uphold the application of strict tort liability law concerning defective products. In strict liability cases, the injured plaintiffs have to prove the product caused them harm but they do not have to prove exactly how the manufacturer was careless. Purchasers of the product, as well as injured bystanders and others with no direct relationship with the product, may sue for damages caused by the product if strict liability is applicable.

Rather than focus on the behavior of the manufacturer (as in negligence), strict liability claims focus on the product itself. Under strict liability, the manufacturer is liable if the product is defective, even if the manufacturer's negligence was not responsible for making the product defective. Because strict liability is a harsh penalty for a manufacturer, who is forced to pay for all injuries caused by its products even if it is not at fault, strict liability is applied only to manufacturing defects (i.e., when a product varies from its intended design) and almost never applied to design and warning defects.

In a strict liability case, an injured party must prove that the product was defective, that the defect proximately caused the injury, and that the defect rendered the product unreasonably dangerous. A plaintiff may recover damages even if the seller has exercised all possible care in the preparation and sale of the product.

Strict Liability for Animals

Traditionally, strict liability has been applied for personal or property damage caused by animals. Because animals are not governed by a conscience and can cause great harm if not restrained, those who keep animals have a duty to restrain them. In most jurisdictions, the general rule is that keepers of all animals, including domesticated animals, are strictly liable for the damage caused when their animals trespass on the property of another. Most statutes, however, make an exception for the owners of dogs and cats, who are not held liable for their pets' trespasses unless they have been negligent or unless strict liability is imposed by statute or ordinance.

For purposes of liability for harm other than trespass (i.e. personal injury), the law distinguishes between domesticated and wild animals. The keeper of domesticated animals, which include dogs, cats, cattle, sheep, and horses, is strictly liable for the harm they cause only if the keeper had actual knowledge that the animal had the particular trait or propensity that caused the harm. The trait must be a potentially harmful one, and the harm must correspond to the knowledge. In the case of dogs, however, some jurisdictions have enacted statutes that impose absolute liability for dog bites without requiring prior knowledge of the dog's viciousness.

Keepers of species that are normally considered wild in that region are strictly liable for the harm these animals cause if they escape, regardless of whether the animal in question is known to be dangerous. Because such animals are known to revert to their natural tendencies, they are considered to be wild no matter how well trained or domesticated they are.

Hypothetical Case

Sandbag Construction Company constructs buildings for commercial enterprises in San Francisco, California. Sandbag knows its tallest building is unlikely to survive a moderate earthquake due to its design and the quality of the soil on which it is built. The company does nothing about this, and when a moderate earthquake strikes, the top floors of the building collapse, killing hundreds of people. Other occupants of the building are trapped for days in the wreckage and suffer serious physical and psychological damage as a result. Can strict liability be imposed on Sandbag Construction Company in this situation? Why or why not?

Chapter 12
Product Liability

Introduction

What is product liability? *Product liability* is the law that holds manufacturers, distributors, wholesalers, suppliers, retailers, and others who make products available to the public responsible for the injuries those products cause.

The claims most commonly made in product liability cases are negligence, strict liability, breach of warranty, and consumer protection statutory claims. Most product liability cases are tried at the state level, and the elements necessary to prove them vary from state to state. Usually, a products liability claim is based on one or more of the following causes of action:

- Design defect
- Manufacturing defect
- Failure to warn

These claims may succeed even when products were used incorrectly by the consumer, as long as the misuse was foreseeable by the manufacturer.

Typically, product liability claims are based not on negligence but on strict liability. Under strict liability laws, a manufacturer is held liable regardless of whether it acted negligently. Strict liability allows recovery for an injured party who might not be able to prove what a manufacturer did or did not do wrong in the design or manufacturing of its product. The law presumes that a manufacturer with deep pockets is in a better position to absorb the cost of liability and that this expense is factored in when setting the price for its products.

In addition, some state laws allow claims based on the manufacturer's failure to warn of a product's dangers. These claims are based on negligence.

As discussed in greater detail in Chapter 10, a negligence claim consists of the following:

- A duty owed the defendant
- A breach of that duty
- An injury
- A breach of the duty owed proximately caused the plaintiff's injury

Strict liability cases are not dependent on how careful the plaintiff was in using the product. In product liability cases, a defendant is liable when its product is proven to be defective. Whether the manufacturer or supplier exercised great care in designing and manufacturing its product is irrelevant. If the plaintiff can demonstrate that there is a defect in the product that caused him harm, the company will be liable for it.

The law of product liability is found mainly in common law and in the Uniform Commercial Code (UCC). Article 2 of the UCC deals with the sales of goods and it has been adopted by most states.

What Makes Up a Product Liability Claim?

In general terms, the law requires that a product meet the ordinary expectations of the consumer. When a product has an unexpected defect or danger, the product does not meet the ordinary expectations of the consumer. There is no federal product liability law, so product liability claims are based on state laws and brought under the theories of negligence, strict liability, or breach of warranty. In addition, a set of commercial statutes in each state, modeled on the Uniform Commercial Code, will contain warranty rules affecting product liability.

Responsible Parties

For product liability to arise, the product must have been sold in the marketplace. In the past, a contractual relationship, known as *privity of contract,* had to exist between the person injured by a product and the supplier of the product in order for the injured person to recover. However, in many states today, that requirement no longer exists and the injured person does not have to be the purchaser of the product in order to recover damages if the product injures them. Any person who foreseeably could have been injured by a defective product can recover for his or her injuries, as long as the product was sold to someone.

Liability for a product defect could rest with any party in the product's chain of distribution, such as the manufacturer, wholesaler, a retail seller of the product, and a party who assembles or installs the product. For strict liability to apply, the sale of a product must be made in the regular course of the defendant's business. Thus, someone who sells a product at a garage sale probably would not be held liable in a product liability lawsuit.

Types of Product Defects

Under any theory of liability, a plaintiff in a product liability case must prove that the product that caused his or her injury was defective, and that the defect made the product unreasonably dangerous. There are three types of defects that might cause injury and give rise to manufacturer or supplier liability: design defects, manufacturing defects, and marketing defects. Design defects are present in a product from the beginning, even before it is manufactured. It occurs because something in the design of the product is inherently unsafe. Manufacturing defects are those that occur in the course of a product's manufacture or assembly. Finally, marketing defects are flaws in the way a product is marketed, such as improper labeling, insufficient instructions, or inadequate safety warnings.

Design Defects

A design defect is some flaw in the intentional design of a product that makes it unreasonably dangerous. Thus, a design defect exists in a product from its inception. For example, a vehicle that is designed with only three wheels might be considered defectively designed because it tips over too easily. Design defect claims often require a showing of negligence; however, strict liability may be imposed for an unreasonably dangerous design if the plaintiff can present evidence that there was a cost-effective alternative design that would have prevented the risk of injury. In some cases, if a product was so unreasonably dangerous that it never should have been manufactured, the availability of a safer design might not be necessary to hold the designer liable.

Manufacturing Defects

A product has a manufacturing defect when the product does not conform to the designer's or manufacturer's own specifications. Manufacturing defect cases are often the easiest to prove because the manufacturer's own design or marketing standards can be used to show that the product was defective. Still, proving how or why the flaw or defect occurred can be difficult, so the law applies two different doctrines in product liability cases to help plaintiffs recover, even if they cannot prove a manufacturer was negligent.

The first doctrine, known as *res ipsa loquitur,* shifts the burden of proof in some product liability cases to the defendant. *Res ipsa loquitur* is a Latin term that means "the thing speaks for itself." It stands for the proposition that the product defect would not exist unless someone was negligent. When the doctrine is successfully invoked, the plaintiff is not required to prove how the defendant was negligent; rather, the burden shifts to the defendant, who is required to prove that it was *not* negligent.

The second rule that helps plaintiffs in product liability cases is that of strict liability. If a statute imposes strict liability, the plaintiff does not need to prove that a manufacturer was negligent but only that the product was defective. By eliminating the issue of manufacturer fault, the concept of no-fault, or "strict," liability allows plaintiffs to recover where they otherwise might not. A manufacturer may be found liable in strict liability cases even if the defendant's misuse of the product caused the injury if it can be demonstrated that a reasonable person would or should have foreseen that the product could have been misused in such a way.

Marketing Defects

Marketing defects include improper labeling of products, insufficient instructions, or the failure to warn consumers of a product's hidden dangers. A negligent or intentional misrepresentation of a product may also give rise to a product liability claim. Manufacturers are expected to warn of any foreseeable dangers in using its product, even dangers that arise from the foreseeable misuse of its product.

Unavoidably Unsafe Products

There are some products that simply cannot be made totally safe without losing their usefulness. For example, a chainsaw that is made completely safe so it could never injure anyone would be useless for its intended purpose. For these products the law assumes that users and consumers are in the best position to minimize their risk of injury. Thus, while a product might not be deemed unreasonably dangerous, manufacturers and suppliers of unavoidably unsafe products must give proper warnings of the dangers and risks their products pose so that consumers can make informed decisions concerning whether or not to use them.

Common Defenses to Product Liability Claims

A defense often raised in product liability cases is that the plaintiff has not sufficiently identified the supplier of the product that allegedly caused the injury. A plaintiff must be able to connect the product with the party(ies) responsible for manufacturing or supplying it. There is an exception to this rule, known as the *market share liability exception,* which applies in cases involving defective medications. Where a plaintiff cannot identify which of the pharmaceutical companies that supply a particular drug supplied the drug he or she took, each manufacturer will be held liable according to its percentage of sales in the area where the injury occurred.

Another defense a manufacturer might raise is that the plaintiff substantially altered the product after it left the manufacturer's control and that this alteration is what caused the plaintiff's injury.

Finally, if a plaintiff misused the product in an *unforeseeable* way, and it is this misuse of the product that caused their injuries, the defendant may be absolved of any liability.

Products Liability and Strict Liability

Many states have enacted comprehensive products liability statutes. These statutory provisions can vary greatly. The U.S. Department of Commerce has promulgated a Model Uniform Products Liability Act (MUPLA) for voluntary use by the states and several have adopted it. There is no federal products liability law. Most products liability claims are not based on negligence but, rather, on strict liability. Strict liability is discussed in greater detail in Chapter 11.

Product Liability and Breach of Warranty

Warranties are statements by a manufacturer or seller concerning a product purchased during a commercial transaction. Unlike negligence claims, which focus on the manufacturer's conduct or strict liability claims, which focus on the condition of the product, warranty claims focus on how these issues relate to a commercial transaction. Warranty claims commonly require privity between the injured party and the manufacturer or seller. Breach of warranty-based product liability claims usually focus on one of three things: (1) breach of an express warranty, (2) breach of an implied warranty of merchantability, or (3) breach of an implied warranty of fitness for a particular purpose. Additionally, claims involving real estate may take the form of an implied warranty of habitability. Express warranty claims focus on express statements by the manufacturer or the seller concerning the product (e.g., "This computer can run three programs at once"). The various implied warranties cover those expectations common to all products unless they are specifically disclaimed by the manufacturer or the seller.

Example

Mike bought a bottle of hair dye from Wally's Drug Store to color his gray hair. As soon as he put the dye on he received a phone call. Mike talked on the phone for half an hour longer than the instructions said to leave the dye on. By the time he hung up the phone, his head was burning, and when he washed the dye off it took his skin with it. Mike spent several days in the hospital, followed by years of surgery to repair the damage—and he was permanently bald. Mike hired an attorney to file a product liability lawsuit against the manufacturer of the hair dye. Mike contended that the hair dye manufacturer failed to warn consumers about the dangers of leaving the product on for more than the recommended five minutes.

The first consideration for Mike and his attorney is a design flaw. Was there something inherently dangerous about the components of the hair dye product? Product liability starts with the very first component providers, which in this scenario would be the chemicals used. Mike's attorney would have to prove that chemicals used were inherently dangerous and the company was aware of this and did nothing to correct it. Product liability lawsuits claiming design defects are notoriously difficult to prove, since many companies spend months or years testing their designs and products before releasing them to the public.

Mike's case might also be considered a manufacturing defect. The chemicals used may have been acceptable but the dye company's manufacturing process may have used too much of them or combined them in a way that made them toxic. Many product liability lawsuits are based on defects caused by poor manufacturing practices or a lack of quality control. The plaintiff's attorney may have to provide expert testimony on the proper construction of a product and compare it with the defective product that caused the injury or damage.

In Mike's case, it would have to prove that the chemicals used in Mike's hair dye were significantly stronger than industry standards. This is how many product liability cases based on manufacturing defects are won.

The third line of reasoning involving product liability is called "failure to warn." Companies have a duty to warn consumers about known hazards and dangers surrounding the normal, or even abnormal, use of their products. Usually, a warning label is placed in a conspicuous area of the product or accompanying literature, which details the known hazards. Some of these warnings may seem obvious, but their presence helps companies defend themselves against product liability claims. In many states, if the plaintiff is even found 1 percent at fault for the accident that caused the harm, the company cannot be held liable.

In Mike's case, his attorney can make the argument that the hair dye company failed to warn consumers that leaving the product on for more than five minutes could result in serious physical injury. Even if Mike's own actions contributed to his injury, some states would allow the argument that the dye company should have included a *Do Not Leave on Hair More Than Five Minutes* warning on the bottle.

Hypothetical Case

Dr. Wizard is a famous heart surgeon who designed a new heart valve that Pacer Company built and sold. Pacer successfully tested the new valve on more than two hundred male patients, aged seventy and older, before marketing the new valve. Many heart surgeons used the Wizard heart valve in their elderly patients. Art Athlete contracted a virus that seriously damaged one of his heart valves, and his heart surgeon replaced it with a Wizard heart valve. Art was an avid runner, and once his doctor told him he was well enough to run again, he began his regime. Six months later, Art ran in the Boston Marathon, but halfway through the race he collapsed and died. An autopsy revealed that the Wizard heart valve had jammed, thus stopping the flow of blood into his heart and causing his death. Art's widow wants to sue Dr. Wizard and Pacer. What will her claims against them be? What defenses will Dr. Wizard and Pacer Co. raise?

Hypothetical Case

Skywalker Mall Inc. builds a skateboarding park as part of its newest and grandest mall complex. The skateboard park is designed by Hudino, one of the premier skateboarders in the country, who comes to the park and christens its opening with a demonstration of his skateboarding skills. During this demonstration, he shows off his newest trick, which is a double backwards flip. The crowd is amazed! Hudino says he was only able to pull of this great feat because of the design of the mall's skateboarding park. He states he constructed it especially so he could get the "air" to do this trick. One of the members of the audience is a 10-year-old boy named Hank, who is an avid skateboarder and fan of Hudino. Two months later, Hank tries to duplicate Hudino's double backflip and crashes. He suffers a broken neck and is paralyzed for life. Hank's parents sue Skywalker Mall Inc. and Hudino, claiming the park's defective design is responsible for their son's terrible injury. What are the arguments for, and against, their lawsuit?

Chapter 13
Criminal Law

Introduction

What is a crime? Typically people think of a *crime* as an act that breaks the law. A crime is that, but it injures more than just the victim; it is a wrongful act that negatively impacts every member of society. Therefore, criminal law differs from civil law because it seeks to punish an individual for wrongs committed against society instead of seeking to compensate a single individual for the breach of a legal duty owed that individual. Thus, the prosecutor in a criminal case represents the "people" of the jurisdiction in which the crime is committed, and punishment and future deterrence is sought on behalf of all the people.

Classification of Crimes

Common law distinguishes crimes in two ways. The first classification is composed of crimes that are innately bad, such as rape, murder, arson, and theft. These are *mala in se* offenses that most everyone agrees are intrinsically and intuitively bad.

The other common law classification is for crimes that are not intrinsically bad but are defined by law as bad. These are *mala prohibita* crimes. Examples of *mala prohibita* crimes are computer crimes, fraud, and a failure to file income tax returns.

In addition to common law classifications, crimes may be distinguished by their victim. Under this approach, crimes are divided as follows:

- Crimes against persons (e.g., rape, murder, assault)
- Crimes against property (e.g., larceny, robbery, arson)
- Crimes against the government (e.g., perjury, contempt, bribery)

Crimes may be further separated according to their severity. Statutes usually classify crimes as either misdemeanors or felonies. Misdemeanors are less serious crimes that, in most jurisdictions, do not entail a punishment greater than one year in jail (typically ninety days is the maximum) and/or a fine of $500. Drunk driving and reckless driving are typical misdemeanor offenses. Felonies are more serious crimes. Punishment for these offenses is usually more than a year in prison and/or a fine greater than $500. Murder, rape, and robbery are examples of felonies.

Each state may define its own crimes and penalties as long as they do so within constitutional limits. In addition, the federal government has its own laws defining crimes.

The Constitution

The Constitution limits the criminal liability and punishment that the federal and state governments can impose on individuals. If a criminal statute is too vague (meaning people can't understand what conduct is prohibited) or overly broad (meaning it makes innocent conduct criminal), the court will rule that it violates the due process clause of the Constitution. For example, a statute would be too broad if its terms were so general it could be used to arrest a person engaged in activities that are protected by the First Amendment (such as operating a blog that criticizes the government).

The Constitution also prohibits the government from enacting ex post facto laws. Ex post facto laws are laws that make acts criminal that were not criminal at the time they were committed. For example, if an individual assisted someone in committing suicide by buying him the ingredients he used to poison himself and there was no law prohibiting this at the time the act was undertaken, then the government could not punish that person later by passing a law prohibiting the act of assisting a suicide. Statutes that imposed a greater punishment or made it easier to prove guilt have also been considered ex post facto laws and declared unconstitutional.

The Equal Protection Clause

The Equal Protection Clause of the Fourteenth Amendment also limits the legislature's ability to define crimes. This constitutional amendment was originally intended to secure freedom from slavery to black people, but it is now used to prohibit state legislatures from passing laws that discriminate against anyone on the basis of their race, religion, or country of origin.

Laws that create classifications based on these categories are subject to strict scrutiny by the courts and can only be justified and enforced if there is a compelling state interest for them. During World War II, the United States removed Japanese American citizens from their homes and put them in isolated camps by declaring them to be a national security risk. Although this reason was accepted as a compelling state interest at the time, it has since been declared constitutional and unacceptable.

Components of a Criminal Offense

When determining if a criminal offense has been committed, there are typically a number of things a prosecutor looks for:

1. A wrongful act (*actus reus*)
2. A guilty mind (*mens rea*)
3. Concurrence (Concurrence happens when a wrongful act is combined with a wrongful state of mind.)
4. Causation

The Wrongful Act

The wrongful act is usually defined by statute. For example, in a battery the wrongful act is the unjustified, offensive, or harmful touching of another person. Sometimes the law classifies a failure to act as a wrongful act worthy of criminal punishment. This happens when the law recognizes a legal duty to act—such as registering with Selective Service, registering firearms, or a parent's duty to care for a child. The law also distinguishes between acts that are classified as voluntary, such as punching a person, and acts that are reflexive, such as epileptic seizure.

The U.S. Supreme Court has ruled that *status crimes,* or making it criminal for a person to have a certain status, are unconstitutional. That is why it is a crime to possess or use controlled substances but it is not crime merely to be a "drug addict."

The Guilty Mind (*mens rea*)

Most criminal convictions require that the defendant possess a guilty mind at the time the crime is committed. A guilty mind may be demonstrated by showing a person had the intent to commit the crime.

Mens rea is often difficult to prove, and the prosecution must often rely on circumstantial evidence to do so. In such instances, the court will instruct jurors that they can assume a defendant intends the natural and probable consequences of his or her deliberate acts.

Common law recognizes three categories of intent:

1. General intent
2. Specific intent
3. Criminal negligence

In general intent crimes, the prosecutor must prove the defendant intended to commit the wrongful act and that he intended the consequences of those deliberate acts. The court will instruct the jury that intent can be inferred from the defendant's conduct.

In specific intent crimes, conviction requires proof of the commission of an *actus reas* (wrongful act) and a specified level of knowledge or an additional intent, such as an intent to commit a felony. For example, a person who possesses a controlled substance with the intent to sell it may be guilty of a specific intent crime.

In criminal negligence crimes the law creates a crime that results from the creation of an unconscious risk. For example, people who willingly drive intoxicated and who cause an accident that injures or kills someone may be convicted of criminal negligence in addition to other drunk driving offenses.

Concurrence

For a successful conviction of some criminal offenses, it is necessary for the prosecutor to not only prove that the defendant committed a prohibited act, but also that the defendant had a guilty mind at the same time. Thus, there is a concurrence between the criminal act and the criminal intent.

Causation

In any criminal case where proving causation is an element of the crime, the prosecution must establish it beyond a reasonable. A key to establishing causation is the legal concept of *proximate cause.* Criminal liability can only attach to conduct that is determined to be the proximate or legal cause of the harmful result.

Proximate cause in the criminal context is similar to that used in tort cases. It says that defendants can only be held responsible for the "foreseeable" consequences of their acts. Thus, just as in the tort realm, it means a defendant cannot be held liable for consequences that follow an intervening, new, or independent causal force.

Strict Liability Crimes

Strict liability crimes are those where the law imposes criminal liability without requiring a guilty act and a guilty mind. To be convicted of a strict liability crime, the prosecutor needs only to prove the defendant committed the prohibited act. It is not necessary to prove the defendant had any criminal intent. These are always statutorily defined crimes. An example of a strict liability criminal offense is the prohibition against selling liquor to minors. If the prosecutor demonstrates that a person sold liquor to a child, it is not necessary to demonstrate that she knew or intended to break the law by doing so. Intent is irrelevant, and only the fact that she sold alcohol to an underage person is relevant or necessary to demonstrate.

Vicarious Liability

Vicarious liability crimes hold individuals or groups criminally responsible for the acts of another. Under vicarious liability, an employer can be held responsible for the acts of employees. It is this theory of vicarious liability that is used to hold a bar owner criminally liable if one of his or her bartenders serves alcohol to a minor.

Inchoate Crimes

Activities that are undertaken in preparation of committing a crime, conspiring to commit a crime, or soliciting others to assist in the completion of a crime, are called *inchoate crimes*.

Defenses to Crimes

The law recognizes several defenses to criminal charges, and creative defense attorneys often attempt to stretch the application of such defenses or to convince the judge or jury to accept entirely new defenses in an effort to raise a reasonable doubt that will result in the acquittal of their client.

Insanity

The insanity defense is used when the defendant admits he performed the criminal act but denies criminal responsibility for that act. For example, he may admit he killed a person but claim it wasn't murder because the person he killed was possessed by Satan and God told him to kill that person.

Different states apply different tests to determine if a defendant was insane at the time the criminal act was committed. One of the oldest tests, and one still used by many states today, is the McNaughten Rule or Test. The *McNaughten Rule* holds that a defendant is not guilty if he was suffering from a mental disease or defect, and as a result of the mental disease or defect did not know the nature and quality of the act that he was committing. For example, if the defendant thought he was killing Satan instead of a human being, he did not know that what he was doing was wrong.

Irresistible Impulse

In some states, a defendant is not guilty if she knows that an act is wrong and is aware of the nature and quality of the act but cannot refrain from committing it due to an irresistible impulse. A typical use of the irresistible impulse defense is when someone catches her spouse in the act of committing adultery and kills him and/or his lover.

Entrapment

Entrapment occurs when police or other law enforcement officers provide a person, who was otherwise disinclined to commit a crime, with the idea and opportunity to do so. The rationale behind the entrapment defense is that it serves to deter law enforcement personnel from engaging in misconduct by enticing individuals who are not initially inclined to commit crimes into committing them.

Self-defense

Under this doctrine, a person who is not an aggressor is justified in using force upon another if he reasonably believes that such force is necessary to protect himself from the imminent use of unlawful force by the other person. Self-defense recognizes a person's legal right to defend himself and property from others. The doctrine of self-defense allows a person to use reasonable force to defend himself from death or serious bodily harm. The amount of force that may be used depends on the amount of force being repelled. For example, a person is not entitled to use deadly force if the other person merely threatens to punch him. Under the self-defense rule, when the attack has been repelled, the defender does not have the right to continue using force to obtain revenge.

For self-defense to be applicable, a defendant must show four things:

1. The use of force was necessary.
2. The force used was proportional to the threat that was being combated.
3. The belief that harm was imminent was reasonable.
4. The defendant was not the initial aggressor.

Even when being threatened, individuals have a duty to retreat if they are not in their home and it is possible to retreat. When individuals are threatened or attacked within their own home, there is no duty to retreat.

Duress or Coercion

Duress or coercion occurs when a person commits a crime only because the person, or an immediate family member, was being threatened with death or serious bodily harm if he or she did not do as commanded. In duress cases, the defendant knew the act was a crime but had no choice but to commit it. The rationale is that the defendant was not acting of his or her own free will when the crime was committed. Usually, duress is not a viable defense in murder cases. Duress is a difficult defense to establish, since there is almost always some reasonable alternative to committing the crime.

Intoxication

Intoxication is a limited defense to some crimes in some states. Most states distinguish between voluntary and involuntary intoxication. A defendant may not be convicted of a crime requiring specific intent if the intoxication was so severe that the person was incapable of forming the requisite intent for conviction.

Although rare, a situation of involuntary intoxication may arise when someone inadvertently ingests incompatible medications or medications and alcohol that make it impossible to convict her of one of the elements necessary for conviction of the crime.

Consent

Consent is not usually a defense except in violent sporting events or when it negates an element of the offense. Consent is most often used as a defense in rape cases.

Prosecution of Businesses

Since a corporation is considered a person under the law, it may be charged with committing a crime. Since a corporation acts through natural persons, it is those persons who may be held responsible for the criminal acts of the corporation. Thus, corporate executives may be charged personally with crimes as a result of actions they took on behalf of the corporation.

A corporation may be charged for even minor offenses if the wrongdoing was pervasive and undertaken by a large number of employees. For example, antitrust violations, financial fraud, criminal negligence and the intentional violation of environmental laws have all resulted in criminal charges against corporations.

One example of a corporation being criminally prosecuted is that of the Pfizer Pharmaceutical Co. In 2007, Nigeria brought criminal charges against Pfizer for the drug company's role in the deaths of hundreds of children who were treated with an unapproved drug during a meningitis epidemic. According to the indictment, Pfizer used the epidemic as an opportunity to conduct biomedical research experiments on Nigerian children by giving them its new and untested antibiotic called Trovan instead of using already available and effective treatments. Nigeria alleged that Pfizer failed to explain to the children's parents that the proposed treatment was experimental and that they could refuse it. The consequences of this unconscionable corporate behavior were even more devastating than the loss of life it initially caused. Because the distrust of Pfizer and other foreign drug companies was so high after this incident, thousands of Nigerian parents refused to have their children immunized against polio. As a result, Nigeria is now one of the last strongholds of polio.

U.S. Attorney Guidelines for Business Prosecutions

Although states have the power to prosecute businesses criminally, and many do, the federal government is often the entity that charges a business with criminal conduct. The U.S. Office of the Attorney General (OAG) is the agency responsible for federal prosecutions, and it has a guideline it follows when determining whether to bring criminal charges against a corporation and its officers. Seven of the factors the OAG considers when determining whether to bring charges against a business are as follows:

1. The nature and seriousness of the offense, including the risk of harm to the public
2. The pervasiveness of wrongdoing within the corporation, including the complicity in, or condoning of, the wrongdoing by corporate management
3. The corporation's history of similar conduct, including prior criminal, civil, and regulatory enforcement actions against it
4. The corporation's timely and voluntary disclosure of wrongdoing and its willingness to cooperate in the investigation of its agents
5. The corporation's remedial actions, including any efforts to implement an effective corporate compliance program or to improve an existing one, to replace responsible management, to discipline or terminate wrongdoers, to pay restitution, and to cooperate with the relevant government agencies
6. Collateral consequences, including disproportionate harm to shareholders and employees not proven personally culpable
7. The adequacy of noncriminal remedies, such as civil or regulatory enforcement actions

The Racketeer Influenced and Corrupt Organizations Act (RICO)

RICO is a federal law that criminalizes certain acts performed as part of an ongoing criminal organization. It also provides a civil cause of action for those injured by violations of the criminal act. Although originally intended to deal with organized crime, this statute has been used to prosecute a wide range of business individuals and organizations, such as financier Michael Milken, Hells Angels, Major League Baseball, and anti-abortionists.

Under RICO, a person who is a member of an organization that has committed any two of thirty-five state or federal crimes within a ten-year period can be charged with racketeering. Under this law, racketeering activity means any of the following:

- Any violation of state statutes against gambling, murder, kidnapping, murder, robbery, arson, obscene mail, dealing in a controlled substance
- Embezzlement of union funds
- Securities fraud
- Money laundering
- Bringing in, aiding, or assisting aliens in illegally entering the country (if the action was for financial gain)
- Acts of terrorism

Hypothetical Case

Sam Smith was a new hire at Mega Stoneworks, Inc., where he began operating a stone-stacking machine that organized the large paving stones made by the company. Although the machine he operated was equipped with a safety device and guarding system, it had been disabled at management's instruction about two years earlier in order to make it quicker to remove stones that occasionally jammed the machine. The company did not have a program to ensure that the safety device was operational and it provided only cursory safety and hazard awareness training to its employees. The company had no procedures to address safety hazards, and employees were unaware of the dangers their machinery posed. As a result, when the machine Sam was operating became jammed, he jumped down from it and attempted to clear the stone that was stuck. When he removed the stone, the machine lurched forward and its load of stones came crashing down and crushed Sam to death. What criminal charge(s) might Mega Stoneworks, Inc. face as a result of Sam's death, and what facts support the charge?

Chapter 14
Criminal Procedure

Introduction

What is criminal procedure? *Criminal procedure* is the administration of criminal justice from the initial investigation of a crime through trial, sentence, and release. It is the process by which crimes are investigated and defendants are prosecuted. In our system of justice, a court cannot impose a penalty against individuals who have not received notice of the action being brought against them or if they have not received a fair opportunity to present evidence in their defense.

Due Process

An integral part of criminal procedure is ensuring that the defendant has received due process. Due process is mentioned in two places in the U.S. Constitution—the Fifth and Fourteenth Amendments. Due process entails an examination of how and why laws are enforced. It is a right that all persons being charged with a crime in the United States are entitled to, regardless of whether they are United States citizens.

There are two types of due process that the law recognizes and regulates. These are substantive due process and procedural due process. *Substantive due process* examines whether a law is fair. *Procedural due process* examines whether the law has been fairly applied. For example, in a procedural due process question, the court determines if a law is too vague or too broad. In a substantive due process case, the court may determine if the law was fairly applied to all persons. Even if procedural requirements are met, it is possible that substantive due process may make the law unconstitutional. For example, the proper process may have been followed in enacting a law allowing warrantless searches of people's homes, and the police may follow the newly enacted law as required, but if the substance of the law itself violates the procedural guarantees of the Constitution, it may be determined to unconstitutionally violate due process rights.

Some basic due process guarantees include the following:

- The right to a fair and public trial conducted in a competent manner
- The right to be present at one's trial
- The right to an impartial jury
- The right to be heard in one's own defense
- The right to have laws written so that a reasonable person can understand what is criminal behavior
- The right to be taxed only for public purposes
- The right to be fairly compensated when the government takes one's property

Arrests

Police may make an arrest only if they have probable cause to believe that a crime has been committed and that the person they are arresting is the person who committed the crime. An arrest does not require a warrant if the police officer witnesses the illegal conduct or it occurs in a public place with other witnesses who saw it and inform police. Although an arrest must be based on probable cause, this does not mean a police officer is required to observe the act firsthand. Information from reliable sources may be sufficient to draft a written complaint that provides the basis for an arrest warrant. The arrest warrant contains the name of the accused (or a description) and a description of the criminal circumstances alleged. To arrest a person in a protected place (i.e., his own home), a warrant is needed.

Bail

Contrary to what some people believe, the Constitution does not give a defendant an unqualified right to bail. It merely says a person cannot be deprived of liberty without due process of law and that a person has a right to a speedy trial. If there are good reasons, such as a significant risk the defendant will flee the country, a judge may refuse to set bail.

Right to an Attorney

The U.S. Supreme Court has held that an indigent defendant is entitled to a court-appointed attorney at all critical stages of a criminal case. Critical stages are interrogation, line-ups, trial, and sentencing.

Arraignment

A defendant is arraigned shortly after being arrested. At the arraignment, the defendant is advised of the charges as required by the Sixth Amendment to the Constitution. The defendant enters a plea to the charge(s), and if he or she refuses to enter a plea the court will enter a plea of not guilty on his or her behalf. Possible pleas a defendant may enter are guilty, not guilty, or no contest (*nolo contendere*). A no contest plea is a defendant's way of saying, "I'm not saying I didn't do it, I'm not saying I did do it. I'm going to let the court read the charge and police report and decide for itself if I'm guilty." In most instances, since the court will only read the police and prosecutor's information, a no contest plea will result in a finding of guilt and the defendant will be sentenced accordingly.

No contest pleas are often used when defendants may not be able to tell the court what they did (perhaps because they were too intoxicated and can't remember) and when an admission of guilt or a jury conviction could be used against them in a civil case. Unlike a criminal conviction, a no contest plea typically cannot be admitted as evidence in a civil case.

Preliminary Examination

A preliminary examination follows the arraignment, and it is where the prosecution must show that a crime was committed and that there is probable cause to believe the defendant committed the crime. If these two things are established, the defendant is "bound over" for trial. Most of the time, the defendant waives the preliminary examination because the burden of proof is much less than that needed for the prosecutor to prevail at trial and because he or she does not want the prosecutor to see any of the defense strategy. As a result, a preliminary examination is usually held only when the crime charged is very weak, inappropriate, or when the defendant's legal team thinks it can gain an advantage by flushing out the prosecution's strategy.

Plea Bargains

A plea bargain is where charges against a defendant are dropped, reduced, or replaced in exchange for a guilty plea or cooperation with law enforcement. If the prosecutor does not honor the plea agreement or the court does not follow a sentencing recommendation made by the prosecutor, a defendant may withdraw the plea.

Trial

If no plea bargain is reached, then the case will proceed to trial. The Constitution states that a defendant is entitled to a speedy trial, at which the defendant must be presumed innocent. At trial, the prosecution must prove each and every element of the offense or offenses charged and guilt must be established by proof "beyond a reasonable doubt." A reasonable doubt is not *any* doubt, but a doubt that is based on reason and common sense after careful and impartial consideration of all the evidence, or lack of evidence, in a case.

During the trial, the prosecutor presents evidence and has the burden of proving that the defendant committed the crime alleged. The defendant's defense team may cross examine the prosecutor's witnesses, produce their own witnesses, and call the defendant to testify on his own behalf, but the defense cannot be compelled to do so and, in fact, all criminal defendants have a constitutional right under the Fifth Amendment not to be compelled to testify at their trial. The jury is not to interpret a defendant's failure to testify as evidence of their guilt. If a jury cannot agree on whether a defendant is guilty or not guilty, it is said to be a hung jury. If a trial results in a hung jury, the judge will declare a *mistrial,* and the case may be retried at the prosecutor's discretion.

A defendant has a right to a public trial unless the state can demonstrate a "compelling state interest" (such as national security) that justifies having a private trial.

Although the Constitution guarantees the right to a trial by one's peers in significant cases, there is no right to a jury for trials involving "petty" offenses, traffic cases, military trials, or juvenile trials.

During trial the defendant has a right to confront his or her accuser, and a right to cross-examine witnesses who testify against him or her. However, if a defendant's behavior in court is disruptive the person may be removed from the courtroom. If the defendant has fled before or during trial, his or her presence may be waived.

Sentencing

If found guilty, a defendant will be sentenced by the judge, or in some states by the jury. Most states use sentencing guidelines established by statute to ensure consistency and fairness. The Eighth Amendment of the Constitution also prohibits "cruel and unusual punishment," although it does not define what this means.

Writ of Habeas Corpus

The writ of habeas corpus, which translated from Latin means "you have the body," is used to question the legality of a prisoner's detention. The writ is granted when a defendant is able to show that incarceration would violate a Constitutional right.

Search and Seizure

Under the Constitution, all government searches, seizures, and arrests must be "reasonable." *Reasonable* means that the government must have probable cause for all searches, seizures, and arrests.

Probable Cause

Probable cause is necessary when deciding if there is enough evidence to charge a particular individual with the crime or to obtain a search warrant. Probable cause is a reasonable suspicion that a crime has been, or is about to be, committed. It can be based on the suspect's statement or conduct, witnesses' statements, and the experience of the police officer. In some instances, a person's consent may eliminate the probable cause requirement. For example, if a couple agree to let the police search their house, there is no need to obtain a warrant based on probable cause. However, if a warrant is necessary, it must contain a sworn affidavit or sworn live testimony of an officer that describes with particularity the place to be searched, the crime that is being investigated, and the source of the information given.

No search warrant necessary if any of the following is true:

- There is no expectation of privacy.
- The illegal item is in plain view.
- The evidence has been dropped or abandoned.
- A person with authority has given consent to search.
- Preservation of the evidence is necessary.
- A search dog found the evidence.
- It is a border search.
- It is a stop-and-frisk situation.
- It is a search incident to an arrest.
- It is a motor vehicle search.
- There are exigent circumstances.

There are a great many court cases discussing what *exigent circumstances* are. Most of them agree that such a circumstance exists when any of the following are true:

- Evidence will be destroyed.
- The defendant or someone else is in imminent danger.
- A prisoner has escaped.

Evidence

Procedural due process requires that evidence of a crime be gathered properly or it cannot be used against the defendant at trial. Unless evidence is in plain view or it has been obtained by consent, a warrant is necessary to search and obtain it. If the defendant and prosecutor disagree whether evidence has been properly obtained and can be used, the judge will determine its admissibility. In making this determination, the judge will review the process by which the evidence was obtained and determine if it was proper and if the evidence itself is relevant and material.

There are five types of evidence that may be presented at trial:

1. Direct evidence
2. Testimony
3. Circumstantial evidence
4. Demonstrative evidence
5. Scientific evidence

Direct Evidence

Direct evidence is evidence that needs no supporting proof or facts. It speaks for itself. Photographs, documents, audio recordings, and videotapes are all examples of direct evidence.

Testimony

Testimony is evidence offered by the words of a witness under oath. Testimony may be direct observations by a witness or circumstantial observations.

Circumstantial Evidence

Circumstantial evidence, or indirect evidence, is proof of a fact by permitted inference or conclusion. It permits a judge or jury to infer the existence of facts that indirectly lead to the conclusion a party is seeking to prove. Circumstantial evidence can be used in either civil or criminal trials. An example of circumstantial evidence is a line-up identification of the driver a blue Ford Mustang by a witness who saw the driver seconds after a similar vehicle drove away from a bank robbery nearby. Direct evidence, on the other hand, would be testimony of a person in the bank who saw the defendant pointing a gun and robbing the teller.

Demonstrative Evidence

Demonstrative evidence is evidence created to persuade the jury. Examples of demonstrative evidence are charts, video recreations, illustrations, and diagrams.

Scientific Evidence

Scientific evidence is evidence arrived at by scientific processes such as DNA, fingerprints, blood test results, or handwriting analysis. To be admissible in court, scientific evidence must have a foundation and it must be relevant, material, and reliable.

Exclusionary Rule

The exclusionary rule holds that if evidence has been obtained improperly, through an illegal arrest or search, it cannot be admitted at trial. There are, however, exceptions to this rule. If the prosecutor can demonstrate the evidence would have been discovered anyway in a legal way, or that there is an independent source for the evidence, or that law enforcement relied in good faith on a defective warrant, the judge may still allow the evidence to be used.

Interrogation and Confession

Most people are familiar with the term *Miranda rights* and know that it means that defendants' incriminatory statements may not be used against them at trial if they were not advised of this possibility. However, this right only applies to defendants' statements made while in police custody. Statements that are voluntarily made when a suspect is not in police custody have no such prohibition and may be used at trial. In addition, there are a number of exceptions to Miranda rights. Miranda rights are not necessary when statements are made in any of the following situations:

- During traffic stops
- Voluntarily
- To undercover law enforcement officers
- In response to background or routine questions
- During an emergency

For a defendant's confession to be admissible at trial, the prosecution must prove it was voluntarily made. In determining this, the court will look to see if the defendant was free to go when it was made, whether Miranda warnings were given, and whether the confession was the result of any coercion.

Hypothetical Case

Danny's Donut Shop is suspected of being a front for the importation of illegal drugs and the laundering of drug money. However the store does seem to have a lot of customers whose only interest is in buying donuts and coffee. One day while staking out the Donut Shop, Officer Perry sees a foreign-looking individual carrying a brown paper sack who looks furtively around and then enter the back door of the store. He comes out the same door, without the sack, about ten minutes later. Officer Perry calls in the license plate of the vehicle the man drives away in and learns it is a rental car. The next day, Perry and his partner are again parked in their unmarked car and they see the same man enter the back of the store. This time he's carrying a black garbage bag. Shortly after the man leaves, Perry decides to go into the store and see if he can find out what was in the bag. When he enters the donut shop the woman at the counter yells into the back room, "Danny, it's a cop." Perry sees a young man grab a black garbage bag and throw it in the walk-in freezer. The man then comes out front and asks Perry how many free donuts he wants. Perry says he wants what's in the plastic bag that Danny just threw in the freezer. Danny says he doesn't know what he's talking about, but the counter clerk says, "No problem, officer, I'll get it for you," and she goes and gets the bag. She hands it to Perry, and inside he sees what turns out to be several kilos of cocaine and at least $50,000. Perry immediately arrests Danny for possession of cocaine and money laundering. What due process arguments can be made in Danny's defense? What facts and arguments will the prosecution make to counter them?

Chapter 15
Real Property

Introduction

What is property? *Property* may be something tangible or intangible, but all property has in common the ability of the owner to exercise control over it. Owners may give property to others or use it in any way they see fit so long as the use does not violate the law. Real property refers to land and all the things that are permanently attached to it, such as trees, buildings, and mobile homes. Anything that is not real property is considered personal property.

Property laws are some of our oldest laws and have helped determine history. Contrast old English with French property inheritance systems. In England, the inheritance system of primogeniture required land held by a person who died without a will to go in its entirety to the eldest son in the family. Widows were not heirs of their husbands. A widow was entitled only to her "dower" rights of one-third of her husband's personal property and the use of one-third of his real property during her lifetime. After her death, the property went to the husband's legal heirs (his oldest son, if he had one).

France used gavelkind. In *gavelkind,* property is divided equally between all of the deceased property owner's sons or male heirs. This meant the property being conveyed would be smaller in each successive generation. Whereas primogeniture retained large land holdings whose owners were wealthy, gavelkind resulted in many small estates whose owners were not wealthy. Eventually, the land owned became so small it was not sufficient to support a family. One of the reasons given as a cause of the French Revolution was a large number of poor and starving people who did not have the means to support themselves.

Types of Property

There are four types of property recognized by law:

1. Real property, which consists of land, buildings, subsurface (mineral) rights, air rights, plant life, and fixtures
2. Tangible property, which consists of things like cars, furniture, and animals
3. Intangible property, which consists of things like bank accounts, stocks, and bonds
4. Intellectual property, which consists of copyrights, trademarks, and patents

Most court cases having to do with property concern the use or transfer of real property. A significant part of resolving real property issues depends on the type of ownership interest a person has in the property. An interest in land, which is or which may become possessory, is an estate. There are many different types of estates or interests in land. Since the United States based its property laws on that of Great Britain, the terms used for real property ownership may seem rather antiquated.

Estates in Real Property

This section discusses some of the most commonly used estates in real property.

Fee Simple Absolute

The most common and complete way to own property is *fee simple absolute*. This form of ownership entitles the owner to use the property for any and all legal purposes. It also allows the owner to sell it or transfer it to heirs.

Fee Simple Defeasible

Fee simple defeasible estates are a more limited form of property ownership. In a fee simple defeasible estate, a person's ownership is subject to a condition. If the condition is not met, the property reverts to the previous owner or the owner's heirs. For example, if a person deeds property to the city of Marquette so long as it is used as a public park, and the city stops using it for a public park after twenty years and decides to use it as a parking lot, it has violated the condition of the deed and it can be *defeased* of the property—the property will revert back to the grantor.

Life Estate

A life estate entitles holders of the life estate to use the property during their lifetime. Upon their death, the property goes to the named person or organization that the grantor specified. An example would be if a person deeded property to the National Wildlife Federation but reserved a life estate in it. The person retains the right to use the property for as long as he lives but when he dies, the property goes to the National Wildlife Federation in fee simple.

Tenancy in Common

In a tenancy in common, two or more people own the property at the same time. Each person has an equal interest in the entire property, and each person may sell or transfer their interest.

Joint Tenants

Joint tenants are also concurrent owners, but unlike tenants in common, when one of the owners dies, his or her portion of the property goes to the other joint tenant(s). Joint tenants cannot sell or transfer their interest in the property without the agreement of all the property owners.

Tenants by the Entirety

Tenancy by the entirety is a form of property ownership often used by married couples. In this form of property ownership, when one of the property owners dies, the property automatically goes to the surviving spouse. No will or probate is necessary for this transfer to the surviving spouse to occur. The surviving spouse merely needs to record the death certificate of the deceased partner. If the parties divorce, the property ownership automatically converts to a tenancy in common.

Community Property

The community property form of ownership is recognized by only a minority of states. Most of them are found in the west. This form of property ownership gives a married person automatic joint ownership of any property the spouse acquires during the marriage. Upon divorce, all property so acquired will be divided equally between them.

Leaseholds

Leaseholds are a nonpossessory interest that is usually defined for a term of years. In a leasehold, one party purchases the right to occupy a land or building owned by another for a specific period of time.

Nonpossessory Interests

A nonpossessory interest in land is a right to use someone else's land for some purpose, but it does not include any ownership of the land. There are several different ways a person may have a nonpossessory interest in land.

Easements

An easement is a right to enter onto another's property and use it without taking away the property owner's rights. An example of an easement is to allow adjacent property owners permission to cross the owner's property so they may be able to access their own property. Without such permission, some property owners could find themselves landlocked with no way to access their property without trespassing. Utility companies often have easements so they may enter land they do not own for the purpose of repairing their lines, pipes, or other infrastructure. When a person sells property, all easements are transferred along with the land. Easements go with the land and are not extinguished when property is sold or transferred.

Although easements are usually the result of a grant, giving rights to someone for a particular purpose, they may also be the result of a reservation where the owner conveys the property but reserves the right to enter it for a particular purpose. For example, the grantor may sell his lakefront property but reserves an easement for lake access from the piece of adjacent property he retains.

License

A *license* is a temporary right to use another person's property. A license is not transferred along with the property when it is sold. An example of a license is when a property owner gives permission to a logging company to come onto the owner's property and harvest timber. Once the company harvests the timber, the license automatically expires and it no longer has permission to enter onto the property.

Mortgage

A mortgage is a security interest in real property that is given in exchange for money loaned to purchase the property.

Deeds

When individuals sell their real property, they do so by giving the purchaser a deed to the property. The deed states the type of estate (interest in land) that is conveyed. It contains the name of the buyer and seller and a legal description of the property being conveyed. The type of deed used also indicates the promises the seller is making about the property. The best guarantee about the property a seller can give is to convey title by use of a warranty deed. In a warranty deed the seller is *warranting* or guaranteeing that they have clear title to the property and the legal right and ability to sell it.

The other way to transfer property is by using a quit-claim deed. A quit-claim deed transfers whatever ownership interest and rights to the property the grantor has to convey. By using a quit-claim deed, the seller promises nothing. The buyer gets whatever interest the seller has in the property. For example, if a person gives you a quit-claim deed to the Statue of Liberty, you get exactly the ownership interest the person gave you—nothing! This may not seem like a very good way to obtain property, but it is quite useful when the seller and buyer trust each other and the buyer knows the seller has the ability to convey good title. Often, property transfers between family members are done by quit-claim deed. Quit-claim deeds are also commonly used to disclaim any interest in land someone may have.

Statute of Frauds

The statute of frauds requires that all contracts for the sale of real property be in writing to be enforceable.

Title Searches

A title search determines if sellers have an interest in property they can convey, what restrictions there are on the use of the property (such as easements), and whether any liens exist on the property for things such as mortgages, back taxes, or special assessments. A title search should be conducted whenever a purchaser is buying property. Companies who conduct title searches examine all documents filed with the register of deeds relating to the property being sold. A good title search will disclose true legal ownership and any liens, taxes owed, easements, and licenses on the property. This is important because the buyer may not want to go through with the purchase if the title search reveals the property is on the verge of being forfeited for back taxes or there is an easement on it that the buyer didn't know about.

Recording Deeds and Relevant Documents

In order to make sure an ownership interest is recognized and to make sure a person receives notice of all legal action being taken against the property in which the person has an interest, it is extremely important that all deeds, land contracts, and other documents exhibiting an interest in a property be recorded with the register of deeds. It is the register of deeds office that title companies, the government, and others use when determining property interests and who to notify concerning actions (such as assessments) taken against the property.

Land Contract

A land contract is an agreement to transfer ownership of real property after the purchase price has been paid in full. In this transaction, the seller provides the financing to the buyer for an agreed-upon purchase price, and the buyer repays the loan to the seller in installments. The seller retains the legal title to the property while allowing the buyer to occupy and use it. When the full purchase price has been paid, the seller is obligated to convey legal title to the property to the buyer. If, however, a land contract buyer makes all but the last payment, the buyer has defaulted on the contract and the seller gets to keep all the money paid and does not have to transfer ownership.

Adverse Possession

The doctrine of adverse possession allows people who have continuously used property under specified circumstances to obtain legal title to it. Under most state laws a successful claim of adverse possession must prove four things:

1. Claimant had sole physical possession of the property.
2. Claimant's possession is open and notorious.
3. The claim is adverse to the real owner. (The claimant has acted as if the property is his.)
4. Possession has been continuous for the required statutory period (usually fifteen or twenty years).

Even if all of the criteria have been met, a person cannot adversely possess government property.

Quiet Title Action

A lawsuit brought to establish a party's title to real property against all other persons is called a *quiet title action*. For example, if a person seeks to obtain title to a piece of property through adverse possession, he would do so by filing a quiet title action.

Nuisance Claims

Sometimes people use their property in a way that annoys their neighbors or interferes with their ability to use or enjoy their property. Claims against property owners that seek to eliminate these problems are based on a nuisance theory and are called *nuisance claims*. There are two types of property nuisance claims.

The first is a private nuisance. A *private nuisance* is one where the annoying or improper use of someone's property only affects their immediate neighbors and not the public. An example would be where a homeowner positions drain spouts so they empty into the neighbor's yard and the runoff forms a pond on the neighbor's property that breeds mosquitoes.

The second type of property nuisance is a public nuisance. A *public nuisance* is when a property use adversely affects a large number of people (the public at large) and involves the general health, safety, or welfare of the public. A public nuisance invokes the police power of the state, and the government may take action to eliminate the problem. An example of a public nuisance would be a property owner who pours large quantities of used oil into a lake that is used by the public.

Eminent Domain

Eminent domain is the power of the government to take private property for a public use. This power is granted by the Fifth Amendment of the Constitution. Eminent domain requires that whenever the government takes private property, it compensates property owners fairly for the "taking" of their property. Usually, this means the government pays the owners the fair market value of their property.

Each state has its own eminent domain power and may delegate that power to some types of public and private companies, typically utility companies, so they can use it to acquire property for the placement of their telephone, power, water, or gas lines.

If a business is operating from real estate that is condemned under eminent domain, the owner is ordinarily entitled to compensation for the loss or disruption of the business resulting from the condemnation, as well as compensation for the value of the property itself.

In a minority of jurisdictions, the owner may also be entitled to compensation for the loss of the business's *goodwill,* which is the value of the business in excess of the fair market value of the real estate due to such factors as its location, reputation, or good customer relations.

The definition of *public use* as interpreted by many state courts has been expansively defined to include anything involving the public's safety, health, interest, or convenience. This has resulted in criticism that some state and local governments are using eminent domain for the benefit of developers or commercial interests and not the public. However, many local governments justify taking private property for business developments on the basis that anything that increases the value of land in its jurisdiction is a sufficient public use.

Zoning

Zoning laws govern where businesses can be located, the size of the lot required for the building proposed, how big the building can be, and other land use issues. All states now have "enabling" statutes that allow them, and local governments, to regulate how land in their jurisdiction may be used. The burden is on property owners to know what uses of their property that zoning laws allow. For example, if a couple wanted to operate a dog grooming business out of their home, they would have to make sure the zoning laws (ordinances) of their city allowed such a use of residential property.

Hypothetical Case

Sally tells Sam she has a great lakefront property lot that she is willing to sell him at a significantly reduced price. Sam asks to see it, so Sally drives him to a spot on a nice lake and paces out what she says are the property lines. Sam agrees to buy the property for $100,000. A week later, Sam delivers the $100,000 to Sally and she gives him a quit-claim deed to the property. About six months later, Sam learns that Sally has left town and she did not own the property she sold him. What legal causes of action does Sam have?

Chapter 16
Personal Property and Bailments

Introduction

What is personal property? *Personal property* in the common law system is often referred to as chattels or personalty. Personal property is distinguished from real property because it is something that can be moved from one place to another. However, just as with real estate, ownership of personal property entails the right to transfer it to another person. The law concerning personal property deals with the rights and relationships among people concerning these things.

Types of Personal Property

There are two types of personal property. The first is tangible personal property, which is any type of property that has physical substance and can be moved. Examples of tangible property are furniture, clothing, books, and jewelry.

The other form of personal property is intangible property. Intangible property is property that has no physical presence and cannot be moved. Examples of intangible property are stocks, bonds, securities, and negotiable instruments. Both types of personal property may be transferred at death by will or disposed of by their owner during life.

Taxation of Personal Property

Some jurisdictions place a tax on personal property, which is an annual tax on the possession or ownership of personal property within the boundaries of the jurisdiction. Automobile and boat registration fees are a form of personal property tax. Most household goods are exempt from this tax as long as they are kept or used within the household. Most often, the tax is placed on expensive personal property such as art or jewelry.

Gifts

A gift is a voluntary transfer of property without any requirement of compensation. Under common law, a gift must meet these conditions:

- The donor (person giving the gift) intends to give a gift.
- The donee (person getting the gift) accepts the gift.
- The item to be given as a gift is delivered to the donee.

Whether something is a gift is important under common law, because contracts are enforceable and gifts are not. Thus, under common law, a promise to make a gift in the future is legally unenforceable even if the promise is accompanied by a present transfer of the physical property that is the gift.

The person who makes a gift (donor) must have a present intent to make a gift of the property to the other person (donee). For example, if your friend gives you an MP3 player and tells you that it's for your next birthday and you are to keep it until then, your friend has not made a gift—there is no present intent to give it to you, and your friend could legally demand the MP3 player back on the day before your birthday. However, if your friend gives you a deed to a piece of property and tells you to keep it in your safe-deposit box, he has given you a gift of the property and would be unable to legally reclaim it. This is because the deed represents the property and it was intentionally delivered to you. A gift must be delivered to the donee. If the gift is of a type that cannot be delivered in the conventional sense, such as real property or a bank account, the delivery can be effectuated by "constructive" delivery. Constructive delivery is when a tangible item that gives access to the property, such as a deed or the key to a house, is delivered instead.

Bailment

What is bailment? *Bailment* is "the rightful possession of goods by one who is not the true owner for a limited purpose." (Williston on Contracts, § 1032) Bailment allows someone who is not the owner of property to exercise possession, power, or control over it and to exclude others from interfering with it.

There are several different forms of bailment:

- *Bailment for the sole benefit of the bailor.* One example would be asking someone to housesit while you are out of town. Typically this situation benefits the homeowner and not the person taking care of the house.
- *Bailment for the sole benefit of the bailee.* One example would be borrowing your neighbor's lawn mower. In this situation the person getting to use the lawn mower is the only one who benefits.
- *Bailment that is a mutual benefit to both the bailor and bailee.* One example would be paying to valet park your car at a restaurant. In this situation the restaurant makes some money while the car owner benefits from having someone else park their car.

For a bailment to exist, there must be a delivery of the personal property that gives the bailee exclusive possession of the property, and the bailee must knowingly accept the bailed property.

Standard of Care Owed in Bailment Situations

When a bailee is entrusted with the care of another's property, the law imposes a duty on the bailee to take good care of the property placed in his possession. The standard of care applied to the bailee differs, depending on the object entrusted and the circumstances of the situation. In some situations, it may be slight care, in others ordinary care, or in some cases, extreme care. For example, the duty may be slight if the property entrusted is a plant that needs watering, greater if it is a cat that needs feeding, and extreme if it is a $100,000 automobile.

To prove that a bailee has failed in his duty of care, the bailor must prove that:

- The bailor surrendered the goods to the bailee.
- The goods were undamaged before the bailor surrendered them.
- The goods were damaged when the bailee returned them.

Use of Goods by Bailee

If there is an express agreement between the bailor and the bailee concerning the bailee's use of the property, then the use is governed by the agreement. If there is no express agreement, then the rules of reasonable use apply. If goods are damaged while bailed, the burden of proof is on the bailee to show he or she did not violate the duty of care. If the bailee converts, sells, or damages the goods while they are in his possession, the bailee may be sued for the obvious violation of his duty of care.

Bailee Rights

In some jurisdictions, there are statutes that allow a bailee to acquire title to bailed goods if all statutory conditions are met. An example of this would be a statute that allows an automobile mechanic to obtain title to a car left in his shop for repairs if the owner never comes back to pay for the work done and retrieve the vehicle.

Finders of Lost Property

People who find objects that are not theirs may be deemed a *finder* or an involuntary bailee. Most jurisdictions do not consider finders to be involuntary or "gratuitous" bailees because they consider there to be some benefit to the finder from the property they possess. A person who finds an object has no obligation to take it into her possession, but if she does, she become a bailee to the true owner of the property with a duty to take appropriate care of it. For example, if you find a stray dog and take it home, you have a duty as the bailee to take good care of the dog for the true owner.

Generally, a finder has title to found property against all but the true owner and prior possessors of it. Typically, if property is found in a public place, the rule is that the finder may keep it if no owner is identified. However, if the property is found on private property, then the owner or occupier of the property is entitled to it.

If a person is acting within the course of his or her employment when a lost object is found, there is a split of opinion in the courts. The majority of courts say the employee may keep the item if the owner is not found. The minority of courts hold that it goes to the employer.

Property is considered abandoned if someone voluntarily left it behind with no intent to retrieve it. In such instances, it is treated the same as if it were lost property.

Treasure trove refers to property that the rightful owner has concealed with the intent to recover it at a later time. This was a rule more commonly used when pirates were known to hide their ill-gotten treasure. Under the British rule, something of value that is hidden in the earth goes to the crown (government), but under the U.S. rule it goes to the finder.

Hypothetical Case

Sam went on a business trip to California. He drove his own car on the trip and checked into the Nice Hotel. The hotel has a guarded underground parking lot. Sam gave his car keys to the parking attendant but failed to notify the attendant that his $5,000 golf clubs were in the trunk. The next day, when he checked out of the hotel, he discovered that his car had been stolen. Sam wants to hold the hotel liable for both the car and the golf clubs. Under what legal theory may Sam attempt to hold the hotel liable? How successful do you think he will be on each claim, and why?

Chapter 17
Contracts

Introduction

What is a contract? A *contract* is an exchange of promises between parties that the law will enforce. The basis of every contract is an agreement. In an agreement, one party makes an offer and the other party accepts it. To reach an agreement, the parties must have a "meeting of the minds." To have a meeting of the minds, the parties must understand each other and intend to reach an agreement. In addition, there must be something of value that is exchanged between the parties. The thing that is bargained for is the consideration for the contract.

Sources of Contract Law

There are three sources of contract law in the United States:

1. Common law
2. Uniform Commercial Code (UCC)
3. Restatement of contracts

Common law developed the equitable doctrines of express and implied contracts, quasi-contracts, promissory estoppel, and unjust enrichment. These doctrines are used to ensure a fair resolution of claims even when all of the elements necessary to make a legal contract are not demonstrated.

The Uniform Commercial Code governs commercial transactions for the sale of goods, negotiable instruments, and secured transactions.

The Restatement of Contracts is a legal treatise written by scholars who are experts in the field of contract law.

The Components of a Contract

There are three basic components of a contract:

1. Offer
2. Acceptance
3. Consideration

The Offer

An offer is an act or statement that proposes definite terms and permits the other party to create a contract by accepting those terms. It is a manifestation of intent to be contractually bound upon acceptance by another party. It is not enough for the offeror (person making the offer) to intend to enter into an agreement. The terms of the offer must be definite. An offer creates in the offeree (person receiving the offer) the power to form a contract by accepting the offer. For example, if your neighbor tells you, "I will pay you $50 if you agree by Thursday to mow my lawn this Saturday," he has given you the authority to create a contract by saying, "I agree," by Thursday.

Termination of Offers

An offer may be terminated anytime before it is accepted. If the offer is revoked prior to acceptance, there is no contract. An offer may also be rejected by the offeree. If a person makes a counteroffer, it is considered a rejection of the offer and is itself an offer.

Acceptance

Traditionally, the nature of the contract has dictated whether the offer can be accepted by a return promise or by actual performance of the promised act. To accept an offer, the offeree must say or do something to accept. Acceptance of the offer must be communicated to the offeror for it to be effective. This can be done in person, by phone, e-mail, letter, or fax. The modern and UCC view of acceptance is that an offer invites acceptance *by any means reasonable* under the circumstances, unless it is otherwise indicated by language or circumstances.

Acceptance is considered effective as soon as the acceptance is out of the offeree's control. For example, once a person puts an acceptance letter in the mail or hits the "send" button on an e-mail, a contract has been formed.

It should also be noted that silence cannot be used as acceptance to create a contract. For example, there is no contract if your friend leaves a voicemail message for you that says, "If I don't hear from you by tomorrow, you agree to bring my car from Detroit to Marquette for $500."

Consideration

A promise must be supported by consideration in order for it to be enforceable. Without an exchange of mutual obligations, there is no contract. Consideration is a bargained-for performance or return promise, which is given by one party in exchange for the promise given by the other party.

Consideration is that which is bargained for in the contract. It is something of value that is exchanged between the parties. For consideration to exist, there must be a bargained exchange in which each party incurs a legal detriment. A legal detriment exists where the party engages in an act that the party was not previously obligated to perform, or the party refrains from exercising a legal right. The thing bargained for can be a benefit to the promisor or a detriment to the promisee.

Consideration does not have to be furnished by or to the parties themselves, as long as it is part of the bargained exchange. For example, someone might say, "If you shovel my grandmother's driveway, I'll pay you $25." If you shovel the grandmother's driveway there is a legally enforceable contract because you did something you otherwise would not have done. However, if a person were to say, "When you turn twenty-one, I'll buy you a beer," there is no contract. Why? Because you're going to turn twenty-one regardless of whether someone buys you a beer. You are not doing anything other than what you will do regardless, so there is no bargained-for exchange. If there is nothing exchanged, there is no consideration, and if there is no consideration, there is no contract.

Consideration can be anything someone might bargain for, but for the contract to be legal, the consideration must be legal.

What Makes a Contract Enforceable?

To be enforceable a contract needs four things:

1. *An agreement.* To have an agreement, one party must make an offer, which the other party accepts.
2. *Consideration.* For there to be consideration, something of value must be exchanged between the parties.
3. *Legal subject matter.* For the contract to be legal, it must be undertaken for a lawful purpose.
4. *Parties with capacity.* For the parties to have the capacity to enter into a contract, they must be adults and of sound mind.

In addition, if a contract does not contain enough information that allows the parties to know what is expected of them, it will fail for indefiniteness.

Mirror Image Rule

The mirror image rule requires that acceptance be made on precisely the same terms as the offer. If any term is changed, it is considered a counteroffer. Today, many jurisdictions follow the UCC rule, which is more flexible.

UCC Rule

The UCC dramatically alters the mirror image rule for the sale of goods between merchants. It states that acceptance is valid even when the offeror inserts additional or different terms in the contract. Under the UCC, merchants are treated differently than consumers. If different terms in a UCC-controlled contract cancel each other out, neither term is considered included in the contract.

Illusory Promises

An *illusory promise* is something that appears to be a promise but really isn't one. Thus, it is an illusion, and is no promise at all. Without a valid promise, there is no consideration, and without consideration, there is no contract. For example, if Sally tells Sam she'll sell him her car for $500 if she can't sell it to anyone else for more and Sam says okay, there is no contract. Why? Because there is no consideration for the contract. Sam has not given anything to secure the agreement. Sally may or may not offer him the car for $500 in the future, and since Sam gave nothing in exchange for this there is no consideration.

Also, if one party makes a promise based on something the other party has already done, there is no exchange and there is no consideration that supports a contract. As far as the law is concerned, past consideration is no consideration at all. An example of this would be a promise like, "Since you sacked the quarterback in last week's game, I'll buy you dinner." There is no consideration in this agreement. Nothing was given or bargained for. The service was already performed before the promise was made. As such, the promise was not made with the intention of inducing any act or forbearance.

Contract Doctrines

In some instances, even though all the elements necessary for a legally enforceable contract are lacking, it would be unfair to allow one party to benefit by taking advantage of the other. As a result, common law courts recognized certain situations where fairness required the imposition of an equitable remedy. Promissory estoppel and quasi-contract are two legal docrtrines that courts use when justice requires.

Promissory Estoppel

Promissory estoppel is used when a party thinks it has a contract and can demonstrate both inducement and detrimental reliance. In promissory estoppel cases, the court determines that the only way to avoid injustice is to enforce the promise made, even when there is no real contract. Promissory estoppel allows one party to enforce a promise even though there is no consideration for the contract. For example, if an employer promises an employee it will pay for her health insurance every month if she retires and she retires in reliance on the promise and the employer refuses to pay, the court may enforce the agreement under promissory estoppel even though there was no consideration to make a binding contract.

Quasi-contract

Quasi-contract is used when the plaintiff reasonably expected to get paid for the benefit provided and the defendant knew this. If the plaintiff gave some benefit to the defendant and the defendant would be unjustly enriched if he did not pay the plaintiff for the benefit, quasi-contract may be used to compensate the plaintiff even when there is no legally enforceable contract. For example, if a lawn-mowing company pulled up to the wrong house and mowed the wrong lawn while the benefiting homeowner sat on the front porch and did nothing to tell the company that it was mowing the wrong lawn, the homeowner might be made to pay for the mowing service. It would be unjust to allow the homeowner to retain the benefit of the mowed lawn when they could have, and should have, done something to correct the error. If the homeowner did not know of it, and just came home to a nicely mowed lawn, the homeowner would not have to pay.

Types of Contracts

Contracts can be bilateral, unilateral, express, and/or implied.

Bilateral Contracts

In a bilateral contract, there is an exchange of one promise for another. The offeror makes an offer, which the offeree may only accept by giving a return promise. For example, if a person says, "I'll sell you my snowmobile for $1,500." There is no contract until someone else says, "I agree to pay you $1,500 for your snowmobile." Bilateral contracts are based on the promise to perform an obligation in the future. The failure to fulfill the promise results in a breach of the contract.

Unilateral Contracts

In a unilateral contract, one party makes a promise that the other party can accept only by doing something. In other words, the offer can only be accepted by complete performance of the promise. For example, a person might say, "If I come home from work on December 30 and you've shoveled the snow from my driveway, I'll pay you $20." If the offeree has shoveled the driveway as required, he has accepted the offer by completing the contract and is entitled to $20. If, however, the offeree failed to perform the act, there would not be a breach of contract since no contract is formed until the offeree renders full performance.

Express Contracts

In an express contract, the parties explicitly state all the important terms of their agreement. For example, "I will paint your garage for $500 by October 30 and you agree to buy the paint and provide all brushes, ladders, solvents, and other supplies necessary for the job."

Implied Contracts

In an implied contract, the words and conduct of the parties indicate they intend an agreement. For example, an employer's practice of paying the cost of gas for his pizza delivery employees may result in an implied employment contract to do so.

Hypothetical Case

Sally is an avid art collector who especially prizes contemporary sculpture. She meets an up-and-coming sculptor and asks him if he will make a work for her garden. He tells her he'll make one for her for $10,000. Sally agrees to pay him $10,000 if he can deliver the sculpture to her house in two months. The sculptor agrees. Two months later, the sculptor delivers to Sally a fork, a knife, and a spoon welded to a shovel. He sticks the shovel's handle in the ground and congratulates her on buying one of his finest works. Sally is furious and refuses to pay him. What arguments are there for and against enforcing a contract?

Chapter 18
Contract Legality Issues

Introduction

An earlier chapter discussed how the law requires there to be an offer, acceptance of the offer, and consideration for a contract to exist. But just because there is a contract does not mean the law will enforce it. So what makes a contract legally enforceable? For a contract to be enforceable, the parties must possess the legal capacity to enter into a contract and the consideration for the contract must be something legal. For example, if the bargained-for exchange is an illegal act, such as murder, the law will not enforce it. A gambling contract is another example where the consideration is illegal unless it is specifically authorized by statute. Some states, such as Nevada, do allow gambling contracts to be enforced.

Public policy also makes life insurance policies taken out on someone else's life enforceable only if the beneficiary of the policy has an insurable interest in the insured. An example would be if the beneficiary is owed money by the insured.

In addition, public policy has also resulted in professional licensing statutes, which are designed to protect the public from people unlawfully practicing a profession or trade. In many states, if a person is not licensed to practice a profession or trade that requires a license, the law will not enforce a contract entered into by such a person. However, if a license requirement is merely to raise revenue (such as a building permit) and not to regulate the profession, a failure to get the license will not invalidate the contract. For example, if a licensed builder contracts to build you a garage and he does so but he fails to pull the necessary building permit, you still have to pay him. This is because the requirement to obtain a building permit is not so much to regulate the competency of the contractor but to generate revenue for the city. However, if an unlicensed builder pulls the necessary permit and builds you a great garage, you do not have to pay him under the contract! This is because he does not have a license that certifies he is competent in his trade as required by the state.

Public policy may be used as the rationale to enforce or prevent the enforcement of certain contracts. For example, a contract that induces elected officials to leave office before their term expires will be ruled unenforceable because enforcement would thwart the desire of the electorate.

Other contracts that would be deemed a violation of public policy are those that would restrain trade. A restraint on trade is any agreement that limits trade, sales, or interstate commerce.

Exculpatory Clauses

There are many situations in which one party attempts to eliminate the possibility of being sued as a result of simple negligence or wrongdoing by including an exculpatory clause in the contract that releases it from liability or holds it harmless. Such clauses are referred to as *exculpatory clauses* or *hold harmless clauses*. By agreeing to such a clause, the other party waives their right to sue for such causes of action.

Exculpatory clauses are included in many types of contracts, such as those in which people agree to waive their right to sue for injuries they suffer as a result of playing on an athletic team or when someone agrees not to sue if the dry cleaner loses or damages her clothes. Other examples include a provision in a lease where the landlord says he is not responsible for damage, injury, or loss that occurs on the property, or a clause in a trust agreement that relieves the trustee from liability resulting from any act performed in good faith under the trust.

Exculpatory clauses are likely to be enforced if all of these conditions apply:

- They are between business parties.
- The clause is limited in scope.
- It is prominent.
- The contract language is negotiated, and not merely a form contract.
- The context of the waiver is fair and reasonable.
- The waiver does not involve the release of a right to sue for negligence in the rendering of professional services such as that by a physician, accountant, or lawyer.

Nonenforcement of Exculpatory Clause

Exculpatory clauses are usually not enforced if they eliminate liability for intentional torts. Most jurisdictions consider eliminating the possibility of being sued for intentionally harming someone to be against public policy and therefore will not enforce such a clause.

Courts have also refused to enforce exculpatory clauses when the bargaining power of one party to the contract is so grossly unequal to the other as to put one party at the mercy of the other's negligence, or when enforcing it would be against the public interest.

Unconscionable Contracts

An unconscionable contract will not be enforced. Unconscionable contracts are those where one party has a significant bargaining advantage over the other and the disadvantaged party has no choice but to accept it, even though no reasonable person would do so. It is a contract that is unusually harsh and often "shocks the conscience." In determining whether a contract is unconscionable, the court will examine the commercial setting and the purpose and effect of the clause or contract.

Under the UCC, if a court finds a contract, or any part of it, to be unconscionable, it may refuse to enforce it, enforce only part of it, or limit the enforcement of it so that it isn't unconscionable.

Adhesion Contracts

Adhesion contracts are contracts in which one party has a much stronger bargaining position than the other and is in a position to effectively tell the other party to "take it or leave it." These types of contracts often get tougher scrutiny by the courts, but they are often upheld. When reviewing legal challenges to such contracts, the courts examine whether the disputed term was outside the reasonable expectations of the purchaser and if the parties were contracting on an unequal basis. The reasonable expectation is assessed objectively, looking at the prominence of the term, the purpose of the term, and the circumstances surrounding acceptance of the term or contract.

Fraud or Materiality

A fraudulent statement is one made to induce the other party to enter into the contract while knowing it is false or not knowing it is true. A statement is material if the maker expects the other party to rely on it in reaching an agreement.

Silent Fraud or Fraud by Omission

An act of fraud does not have to be an affirmative act for it to be the basis of rescinding a contract. Silent fraud occurs when a defendant fails to disclose material facts. To establish silent fraud, the plaintiff has the burden of proving each of the following seven elements by clear and convincing evidence:

1. The defendant failed to disclose one or more material facts about the subject matter of the claim.
2. The defendant had actual knowledge of the fact(s).
3. The defendant's failure to disclose the fact(s) caused the plaintiff to have a false impression.
4. When the defendant failed to disclose the fact(s), the defendant knew the failure would create a false impression.
5. When the defendant failed to disclose the fact(s), the defendant intended that plaintiff rely on the resulting false impression.
6. The plaintiff relied on the false impression.
7. The plaintiff was damaged as a result of the reliance on the false impression.

For example, a used car salesman tells Sally the car was a one-owner and it received regularly scheduled maintenance, but he knowingly fails to tell her it was in the owner's garage, which was flooded during the last hurricane. If Sally believes the car is in good shape and buys it based on his assertions but soon after, the body begins to rust and the engine needs repair and her mechanic tells her, "This vehicle has obviously been under salt water." Sally may sue to rescind the sales contract if she can demonstrate these seven things:

1. The salesman knew the car had been flooded with saltwater.
2. He failed to tell her about it.
3. Because he didn't tell her, she got the false impression the car was in good condition.
4. The salesman knew his failure to tell her would cause her to get a false impression.
5. He intended her to rely on the false impression.
6. She did rely on it.
7. She suffered injury as a result of her justifiable reliance.

Justifiable Reliance

Justifiable reliance occurs when the injured party can show he reasonably relied on a false statement that was material to the contract. Thus, if a party can show: (1) a false statement of fact; (2) fraud or materiality; and (3) justifiable reliance, the contract may be rescinded. When a contract is rescinded, it is as if it never took place and the remedy is to put the parties in the same position they would have been in if the transaction never occurred. No rescission is permitted if one party is aware of the risk. For example, if a purchaser buys a painting hoping it was painted by Rembrandt but after taking it to a museum curator he learns that it was not, he cannot rescind the contract merely because the painting was not what he hoped. He knew when he bought it that he was taking a risk that the painting was done by someone other than Rembrandt.

Mistake

What if there is no fraud or intentional act to deceive but merely a mistake? A mistake can be either bilateral (made by both parties) or unilateral (made by one party). A bilateral mistake occurs when both parties rely on the same factual error. A unilateral mistake occurs when one party enters into the contract under a mistaken assumption. The law says that if a contract is based on an important factual error (mistake), it is voidable by the injured party.

To rescind a contract when there is a unilateral mistake, a party must prove it entered into the contract because of a factual error and either enforcing the contract would be unconscionable, or the non-mistaken party knew of the error.

A party that seeks to void a contract due to misrepresentation must show five things:

1. The defendant made a misrepresentation.
2. The misrepresentation was either fraudulent or material.
3. The misrepresentation induced the plaintiff to enter into the contract.
4. The plaintiff's reliance on the misrepresentation was justified.
5. The plaintiff suffered damage as a result.

A *misrepresentation* is an assertion by either words or conduct that is not supported by the facts. A misrepresentation is *fraudulent* if it is both knowingly false and intended to mislead. The maker intends to induce a party to enter into the contract by making a statement they know is not true while intending the party to rely on it. For example, if a used car salesman knows the car has bad head gaskets that need replacing but tells the prospective buyer "this car is in excellent condition" so that she will buy it, he has fraudulently misrepresented the condition of the car. If he was unaware that the head gaskets were bad and made the same statement he would be merely misrepresenting the condition of the car but his misrepresentation would not be fraudulent.

A misrepresentation is *material* if either it is something a reasonable person would attach importance to in making his or her choice of action or the person making the misrepresentation knew it was likely to induce the other party to enter into the agreement.

A party is justified in relying on the misrepresentation unless it is only incidentally important to the contract or unless a reasonable person would not be expected to take the misrepresentation seriously.

A party loses the power to rescind a contract for misrepresentation if, after the party knows of a misrepresentation, the party manifests to the other party an intention to affirm the contract anyway or fails to demonstrate an intent to rescind the contract within a reasonable time.

Note: False representations may be the basis for rescinding a contract if those representations are either fraudulent or material. However, in tort law, a misrepresentation does not result in liability for fraudulent misrepresentation unless it is *both* fraudulent and material.

Undue Influence

A contract made as a result of undue influence can also be rescinded. To prove undue influence, a party must prove: (1) a relationship between the parties of trust and domination, and (2) improper persuasion by the stronger party. The lawyer and client relationship or a medical advisor and patient, may, as a matter of law, give rise to the presumption that undue influence has been exercised.

Hypothetical Case

Sally is on vacation in Arizona and is browsing around a tourist shop when she spies what she thinks is an antique Navajo blanket. She asks the store owner if it is one, and the owner says, "I think it is, but I haven't had a real expert examine it yet." The store owner knows it was purchased from someone who has a reputation for making great-looking fakes, but she says nothing about that. Sally, who knows a bit about Native American rugs, examines the rug more closely and asks how much the owner wants for the rug. "Well, since I can't swear it is an antique, although it has all the indications of being one, I'll sell it to you for $2,000." Sally thinks that's a pretty good price for what she believes is a genuine antique and buys it. When she has an antique Indian rug dealer examine it, he tells her it is a fake and that he knows who made it and where she probably bought it. What cause of action(s), if any, does Sally have against the store owner who sold her the rug? Explain your answer.

Chapter 19
Contract Capacity

Introduction

What does capacity mean when talking about contracts? *Capacity* is the ability of a party to enter into a legally binding contract. To have the capacity to enter into a legally binding contract, a person must be of legal age and have the mental ability to understand the agreement.

Age

To be able to understand the ramifications of entering into a contract, most states believe a person needs to be at least eighteen years old. Anyone under the age of eighteen is a minor, and the law says minors do not have the capacity to enter into contracts. Because minors lack the capacity to contract, their contracts are voidable.

Voidable Contracts

A *voidable contract* is one that exists but may be canceled. By contrast, a *void contract* is one that the law treats as never having existed. This distinction is important because a party to a voidable contract may choose to waive the right to rescind it and decide to abide by it instead. If a contract is void, there is no way it can ever be made enforceable.

A contract in which one party lacks capacity is voidable and may be canceled by the party who lacks capacity. Thus, a minor who lacks capacity has the ability to choose between enforcing the contract or disaffirming it. The other party, however, has no choice and must abide by the contract if the minor decides to affirm it. If a minor decides to disaffirm a contract, he or she must do so within a reasonable amount of time or they will be held to it.

Minors may disaffirm a contract by notifying the other party that they refuse to be bound by it. They may also seek a court order that rescinds the contract. A minor who disaffirms a contract must return the consideration received to the extent he or she is able or compensate the other party for the property that cannot be returned. Restoring the other party to the position it was in before the contract took place is called *restitution,* and minors must make restitution once they disaffirm a contract. They cannot keep the benefit of the bargain while simultaneously disaffirming the contract.

Most states will not allow a minor to disaffirm contracts made for necessities. *Necessities* are such things as food, clothing, housing, and medical care.

Mental Capacity

A party suffering a mental impairment such as dementia or mental illness may seek to void a contract. Just as minors must make restitution when they disaffirm or void a contract, so must those who are mentally infirm.

Intoxication

If a person is so intoxicated he cannot understand the nature or consequences of the transaction, the contract entered into is voidable. This is usually quite a difficult legal argument to successfully make.

Hypothetical Case

Sam is seventeen years old but has been working for two years and saving every dime so he can buy his own car. He finally has $4,000 and goes to a local car dealer. He decides to buy an older-model Jeep for $3,800. When the contract is prepared, the dealer looks at him and says, "You are eighteen, aren't you?" Sam says he is, and the contract is concluded. Sam enjoys driving the car for six months, and then the transmission blows. He's quoted a cost of $2,000 to fix the transmission. When he complains to a friend that he doesn't have the money to fix his car, the friend tells him, "Heck, you're seventeen, so the dealer shouldn't have sold it to you since you can't make contracts. Just take it back and tell the dealer you want your money back." Sam decides he'll do just that. Will he be successful in voiding the contract, returning the Jeep, and getting his $3,800 back? Explain your answer.

Chapter 20
Written Contracts

Introduction

Some contracts are considered so important that the law requires them to be in writing to be enforceable. The law that specifies what contracts must be in writing to be enforced is called the *statute of frauds*.

Statute of Frauds

The statute of frauds defines contracts that must be in writing to be enforced. It also requires that they be signed by the defendant to be enforced. Under the statute of frauds, a contract must be in writing if it fits one of these six criteria:

1. *It is for an interest in land.* Agreements for an interest in land include mortgages, life estates, and leases.
2. *It is to pay the debt of another.* When one person agrees to pay the debt of another as a favor, it is called a *collateral promise,* which must be in writing to be enforced.
3. *It will take more than one year to perform.* For such agreements, the date is calculated from the day the parties make the agreement. If a contract *could* be performed within one year but it actually isn't, that does not invalidate the contract.
4. *The executor of an estate makes the contract.* If the executor of an estate (who makes sure the decedent's debts are paid) promises to pay a decedent's debt out of his or her own funds, it must be in writing to be enforceable.
5. *The goods cost more than $500.* The UCC requires a written contract for the sale of goods worth $500 or more.
6. *It is made in consideration of marriage.* For example, a pre-nuptial contract is a contract made in consideration of marriage in which each party agrees to a pre-determined division of property and assets if the marriage should end in divorce.

Although the statute of fraud requires these six types of contracts to be in writing, if a party renders full performance of its part of the bargain concerning an interest in land, the law will not allow that party to disaffirm it merely because the agreement was not written. Sometimes even when a buyer paid part of the purchase price and either took possession of the land or made improvements to it, the buyer will not be able to avoid the contract just because it isn't in writing.

Another exception to the requirement that an agreement be in writing to be enforced is in situations where promissory estoppel may be applied. Promissory estoppel is used when one party makes a promise that reasonably causes the other party to rely on it, and the other party does act in reliance on it to the party's detriment.

Elements of a Valid Written Contract

A written contract must contain four things:

1. The name of each party to the contract
2. The signature of the defendant
3. The subject matter of the agreement
4. All the essential terms and conditions of the agreement

An agreement must always be signed by the party against whom enforcement is sought. The term *signature* is interpreted loosely. A stamped signature, a logo, or even an "X" have been acceptable as signatures to the court.

The UCC

The key difference between the UCC and the common law rule is that the UCC does not require all of the terms of the contract to be in writing. The two things that remain essential, however, are the signature of the defendant and the quantity of the goods being sold.

There is a *merchant's exception* to the UCC's written requirement. For routine business between merchants, a letter from one merchant to the other confirming an order, which is definite enough to bind the sender, will be an enforceable contract unless the receiving merchant objects to it within ten days.

Electronic Signatures

Under federal and many state laws, an electronic signature can be used to execute contracts. Electronic signatures may be a symbol, sound, retinal scan, or other unique identifier. Electronic signatures are not acceptable for insurance contracts, wills, or medical release forms.

Parol Evidence

The *parol evidence* rule prevents a party to a written contract from contradicting or adding terms to a contract by seeking the admission of evidence that is outside of the contract. Parol evidence is anything outside of the written agreement that was said or done before the contract was signed. Most contracts specify that they contain all the terms and conditions and no other agreements are binding. Rarely, if a court determines that a contract is incomplete or ambiguous, it will allow parol evidence to fill in the missing information.

For example, Sally and Sam enter into a contract in which Sam agrees to paint Sally's house blue for $4,000. Nothing in the contract specifies that Sally is to pay for the paint. When Sam finishes painting the house, Sally gives him a check for $4,000. He says, "Thanks, but you also owe me another $1,000 for the cost of the paint." If Sam sues Sally for the additional $1,000 and tries to introduce testimony that they had an oral agreement that she would also pay him for the cost of the paint he used, the parol evidence rule will prevent the testimony from being admitted.

Hypothetical Case

Sally and Sam negotiate Sam's purchase of Sally's motorcycle. When he agrees to buy it for $1,500, she says, "Great, I'll even throw in the helmet for free." Sally grabs a piece of paper and writes up the following: "Sally agrees to sell Sam her Honda motorcycle for $1,500, payable within seven days." Sam signs the contract and dates it. He returns in three days with the $1,500 and Sally gives him the motorcycle and signs off on the title. Sam says, "Hey, where's the helmet?" Sally responds, "Oh, I gave it to my cousin since he lost his." Sam is really upset, since he doesn't have a helmet and didn't buy one since he thought he was getting Sally's. If Sam sues Sally for breach of contract to get the helmet (or its value), is he likely to prevail? Explain why or why not.

Chapter 21
Third-Party Contracts

Introduction

Sometimes a person or corporation wants to enter into contract that is for the benefit of someone else. Under certain circumstances, these contracts may be enforced by the party who is to benefit from them, even though the beneficiary is not the party providing the consideration for the contract.

Third-Party Beneficiary Contracts

Third-party beneficiary contracts are contracts that are made to benefit someone other than the parties to the contract.

Third-Party Beneficiaries

A *third-party beneficiary* is someone who is not a party to the contract but who will benefit from it. For example, if a city contracts with the bus company to pay the cost of bus fares for people riding it to come and work at a factory located there, the factory is a third-party beneficiary of the agreement because it gets the benefit of laborers it wouldn't otherwise have.

A third-party beneficiary may seek to enforce a contract (to which it is not a party) if it can prove one of three things:

1. It was an intended beneficiary of the contract.
2. Enforcing the contract will satisfy a duty of the promisor to the third-party beneficiary.
3. The promisee intended to make a gift to the beneficiary.

The most common example of an explicit third-party beneficiary is a life insurance policy. In a life insurance policy, the owner is the individual who purchases the policy and is usually the insured life. The insurance company is one of the parties to the contract, and the third-party beneficiary is the named beneficiary who will receive the policy benefits when the insured dies.

Intended third-party beneficiaries of a contract may enforce the contract in court. A beneficiary of a life insurance policy may sue in civil court in his own name to enforce the policy after the death of the insured.

A person who is not an intended beneficiary but who still benefits from the contract is an incidental beneficiary, also known as a *donee beneficiary*. An incidental or donee beneficiary may not enforce the contract because it was not made for their benefit. For example, if the city contracts with ABC Construction Co. to repave Main Street and the local parking garage receives a huge increase in business because people can't park on Main Street during the construction, the parking garage is an incidental beneficiary because it is benefiting from the construction project but the project was not undertaken with the goal of benefiting it.

To determine if a third-party beneficiary may enforce a contract to which it was not a party, the court will examine whether the contracting parties were aware that the third party would benefit and if one of the contracting parties wanted to make a gift to the third party or satisfy an obligation owed.

An intended beneficiary is either a *donee* or *creditor beneficiary*, and acquires rights to enforce the original contract depending on which category of beneficiary they are.

Assignment and Delegation

A contracting party may transfer its rights under a contract. This is called an assignment of rights.

If a party transfers its duties (obligations) under a contract, it is called a *delegation of duties*. It is not uncommon for a party to both assign and delegate at the same time, thus transferring rights and duties to a third party.

Assignment

Any contractual right may be assigned unless one of these three conditions apply:

1. It would substantially change the obligor's rights or duties under the contract.
2. It is forbidden by law or public policy.
3. It is validly prohibited by the contract itself.

Contracts may contain a clause that specifically prohibits assigning rights. These are typically enforced. A common example of this is a provision in a lease that prevents it from being assigned.

A substantial change to the contract itself is one that makes a significant difference in the obligor's duties.

An assignment may be written or oral, but if the statute of frauds is applicable, it must be done in writing.

Once the assignment is made and the obligor is notified, the assignee may enforce the contract against the obligor. An assignment of rights for consideration generally includes an implied warranty that the claim is valid. The obligor is also entitled to raise all the defenses against the assignee that he or she could have raised against the assignor.

Delegation

An obligor may delegate duties unless three conditions apply:

1. Delegation would violate public policy.
2. The contract prohibits delegation.
3. The obligee has a substantial interest in personal performance by the obligor.

Delegation may violate public policy in contracts with a government or its agencies. A contract may itself state that it forbids delegation. Sometimes, even without a nondelegation clause, the court may disallow delegation if the work is of the kind that requires personal performance. For example, if a person hires a particular coach for tennis lessons and the coach says she's delegating the duty to an assistant coach, the delegation would not be enforceable since the contract required specific performance by the contracting coach.

Assignors who are paid for making an assignment are held to make certain implied guaranties about the assignment.

The assignor must notify the promisor of the assignment.

Novation

A *novation* is a three-way agreement in which the obligor transfers all rights and duties to a third party. A novation has the effect of releasing the obligor from liability.

Hypothetical Case

Sam's grandmother is quite elderly but still lives by herself in the same house she has lived in for 40 years. She is in no shape to do yard work, however, and since Sam is too busy to mow her lawn for her he contracts with Larry's Lawn Service and to mow her 100 x 150 foot yard once a week from June through September. He pays Larry's Lawn Service $400 in advance for this year's service. Unfortunately, Sam's grandmother dies the second week of June. As a result Sam tells Larry's, that as the executor of his grandmother's estate he is assigning the lawn mowing contract to himself so Larry's should mow his 200 x 200 foot lawn for the remainder of the contract term. Will Larry's have to mow Sam's yard for the rest of the summer? Why or why not.

Chapter 22
Warranties

Introduction

What are warranties? A *warranty* is a guarantee that an article or service sold is as factually stated or legally implied by the seller. Warranties are promises that the good(s) purchased will perform as the buyer reasonably expects them to.

There are several types of warranties recognized by the Uniform Commercial Code (UCC).

Express Warranty

Express warranties are affirmative promises about the quality and features of the goods being sold. For example, if a company claims that a digital camera is "waterproof to 50 feet," or that a car gets "40 miles per gallon on the highway," these are express warranties.

Express warranties under the UCC include more than just affirmative statements. A description of the goods being sold or samples shown to the buyer also form an express warranty. If the buyer is shown a floor sample of the kind of television he wants to buy, this sample is an express warranty that the television actually sold to him is the same type and quality as the floor sample.

An express warranty can arise in one of three ways:

1. Oral or written representations
2. A detailed description of the product
3. A sample or model creating the impression that all goods will conform to the sample

Note: If the seller gives an express warranty to a buyer, the seller may not legally include language in the contract that disclaims or counteracts the warranty.

Implied Warranty

The UCC also creates a second kind of warranty, called an *implied warranty*. As the name suggests, an implied warranty is made regardless of whether it is specifically mentioned.

The implied warranties created by the UCC ended the old rule of caveat emptor: Let the buyer beware. Implied warranties allow buyers to purchase goods and be confident they meet certain minimum standards.

There are two implied warranties the UCC creates:

1. A warranty of "merchantability" of the goods being sold
2. A warranty that the goods are "fit for a particular purpose"

Implied Warranty of Merchantability

Under the UCC's definition of *merchantability*, goods must be at least of average quality, properly packaged and labeled, and fit for the ordinary purposes they are intended to serve.

For example, a camera would have to be at least of average quality as compared to other cameras in the same price range, it must take pictures, and it cannot come in a package labeled "Nikon" unless it is, in fact, a Nikon camera.

The application of the implied warranty of merchantability is limited to sellers of "goods of that kind," which means the kind of goods the seller usually sells in the marketplace. A seller does not make an implied warranty of merchantability when it sells goods of a kind that it does not normally sell. For example, a store that sells cameras and camera supplies warrants that the cameras it sells are merchantable because cameras are the kind of goods it typically sells. However, if the camera store has a cash register it no longer needs and sells it to the store next door, the cash register is not subject to an implied warranty of merchantability because the camera store does not normally sell cash registers. But if the camera store makes an express warranty regarding the cash register, such as, "This cash register is in excellent shape and will last at least a year," it will be held to that warranty.

Fitness for a Particular Purpose

The implied warranty of fitness for a particular purpose applies if the seller knows, or has reason to know, that the buyer will be using the goods he is buying for a certain purpose. If the seller knows the purpose for which the goods are to be used, the seller impliedly warrants that the goods being sold are suitable for that specific purpose.

For example, a camera salesperson may sell cameras that are suitable for everyday picture taking and therefore they are merchantable. But if the salesperson knows the buyer wants to use the camera to take pictures underwater, the salesperson also impliedly warrants that the camera sold to the buyer is suitable for that purpose.

The rationale behind the implied warranty of fitness for a particular purpose is that buyers typically rely on the seller's knowledge and expertise to help them find the specific product that meets their particular need. A buyer who goes into a hardware store to buy a snowblower relies on the hardware salesperson to find the snowblower that fits his specific requirements. The rationale is that it is unfair to allow a seller to sell something that the salesperson knows will not do the job and later tell the buyer it is not the store's fault it did not work for the purpose purchased.

Limited Liability Clause

Most sellers limit the scope of the warranties they make to avoid liability for as many potential problems as possible. As a result, they will include clauses in their sales agreement that place conditions on the warranties they provide. These warranty-limiting clauses are referred to as *limited liability clauses*.

A limited liability warranty is a warranty with certain conditions and limitations on the parts covered, type of damage covered, and/or time period for which the warranty is good.

Warranty Disclaimers

The UCC specifically allows sellers to disclaim both express and implied warranties on goods they sell, within certain limits. These warranty disclaimers are typically enforced by the courts unless doing so is determined by the court to be unreasonable under the circumstances.

A seller who disclaims a warranty under the UCC must do so specifically. A general statement that there are "no warranties, express or implied" is usually ineffective. How express a disclaimer needs to be depends on the kind of warranty being disclaimed.

An express warranty must be expressly disclaimed. A disclaimer that disclaims the implied warranty of merchantability must specifically mention merchantability in it. If a seller wants to disclaim all implied warranties, the seller should do so by stating that the good is being sold "as is," or by using some other phrase that makes it plain to the buyer there are no implied warranties.

The UCC also requires that all disclaimers of implied warranties be in writing. Hiding a warranty disclaimer in the small print of a lengthy sales contract will likely not be enforced, though, because the UCC also requires that a disclaimer be conspicuous. A section of a contract is conspicuous if it clearly stands out from the rest of the contract and draws the eye of the reader to it. Common ways to make contract provisions conspicuous are to put them in bold type, different colored type, larger type, or in all capitals. Therefore, all disclaimers of warranties should be in writing, should be conspicuous, and should specifically mention the warranty being disclaimed.

Many states require that a buyer have some meaningful remedy if the goods he or she receives are defective so they will not enforce a total disclaimer of all warranties. Just as a disclaimer that is too broad will not be enforced, neither will a disclaimer that takes all rights away from the buyer. In addition, most states have consumer protection statutes for the purchase of consumer goods. These statutes often provide the buyer with remedies other than those provided by the UCC, and also often provide that a consumer's rights under the statute cannot be abridged by means of a disclaimer.

If, after a reasonable opportunity to inspect, the buyer keeps the goods, the buyer will be deemed to have accepted them. The failure to reject goods in a reasonable time constitutes acceptance.

Extended Warranties

In retail businesses, an *extended warranty* refers to a guarantee of the reliability of a product under conditions of ordinary use. It is called an "extended" warranty because it covers defects that arise some time after the date of sale. If the product malfunctions within a stipulated amount of time after the purchase, the manufacturer or distributor typically provides the customer with a replacement, repair, or refund. Extended warranties do not cover the abuse, malicious destruction, or "acts of God" that damage or destroy the product.

Magnuson-Moss Warranty Act

The *Magnuson-Moss Act* is a federal law that outlines the specific guidelines and requirements that manufacturers and sellers must follow. It requires them to disclose detailed information about their warranties to consumers. The act provides consumers protections and the right to receive compensation for defective products, and it requires manufacturers to provide meaningful warranty coverage.

The act contains the "three-strikes" principle, which places a limit on the number of times a manufacturer can try to fix a defect before having to compensate the customer.

Remedies for Breach of Warranty

When the seller has breached an express warranty, there are three options:

1. The buyer can return the product.
2. The seller can replace the product.
3. The seller can have the product repaired.

When a consumer buys an item that is broken or missing pieces before it was even taken out of the package, it is a defective product and can be returned to the seller for refund or replacement, regardless of what the seller's "return policy" might state (this is not true for second-hand or "as-is" sales).

Also, if the product fails prematurely, it may be considered defective when it was sold and could then be returned for a refund or replacement. If the seller dishonors the warranty, then the buyer has a breach of contract claim.

Hypothetical Case

Sam goes to Computer Sales, Inc. and talks to a salesperson about his desire to purchase a new computer that he plans to use in his start-up graphics design business. The salesperson talks him into buying a computer that is on sale. When Sam sets it up in his new office, he finds the machine doesn't have enough memory or speed to run the programs required for his business. What warranty, if any, has Computer Sales, Inc. breached in selling the computer to Sam?

Chapter 23
Remedies

Introduction

What is a remedy? A *remedy* is a method used to compensate the injured party in a lawsuit.

In order to obtain a remedy, a party must be able to demonstrate that it has suffered injury, which entitled the party to claim damages. The court's purpose in assessing damages is to help the injured party without unfairly harming the other. The idea is not to punishing the wrongful party, although in some instances punitive damages are allowed in an effort to prevent others from engaging in similar reprehensible conduct.

When determining what remedy to apply, the first step the court takes is to identify the interest to be protected. An interest is a legal right in something. A person may have a legal interest in property, a contract, or in a personal injury (tort) claim.

The most common remedy in both tort and contract claims is an award of money damages. In order to recover monetary damages, a plaintiff must prove an injury to person or property. For example, if the defendant isn't paying attention and rams the plaintiff's boat, which causes $10,000 in damage to the plaintiff's boat, the plaintiff may sue the defendant for negligence and get a $10,000 money judgment, which compensates for the $10,000 spent getting the boat fixed.

Remedies in Tort

The type of damages one can claim depends on the cause of action alleged. Lawsuits based on a tort claim may seek five types of damages:

1. Nominal damages
2. Compensatory damages
3. General damages
4. Punitive damages
5. Special damages

Nominal Damages

Nominal damages are those awarded when the plaintiff has not sustained an actual loss or injury. Nominal damages are intended as a statement that the type of conduct the defendant has engaged in should not be permitted.

Compensatory Damages

Compensatory damages are also referred to as actual damages. They are awarded to compensate the plaintiff for loss, injury, or harm suffered by the defendant's breach of duty.

General Damages

General damages are noneconomic damages, which are not easily demonstrated. These include things such as pain and suffering or the loss of a bodily function or appearance.

For example, if the defendant negligently causes a fire in the chemistry lab and the plaintiff is burned and disfigured for life, the plaintiff may recover $1,000,000 after demonstrating she has developed a phobia of chemistry labs and she has a horribly disfigured face.

Punitive Damages

If the defendant's conduct is found to be intentional or willful or wanton or malicious, the court may permit an award of punitive damages in addition to compensatory damages

Punitive damages are uncommon and some states do not permit them, but if a defendant's conduct is so egregious, the court may use punitive damages to punish the defendant and to discourage others from engaging in the type of conduct engaged in by the defendant. An example is found in some lawsuits filed against cigarette manufacturers. These lawsuits alleged that cigarette manufacturer's knew that their product (cigarettes) were addictive and caused cancer and other serious health problems and yet manufacturers continued selling them as if they were a benign product. When successful plaintiffs proved they had misled the public about the health risks of smoking cigarettes some courts imposed punitive damages in addition to compensatory damages.

Special Damages

Special damages in tort cases consist of medical expenses, in-home medical care, loss of wages, and the loss or impairment of future earning capacity. Special damages, which are sometimes referred to as economic damages, are measured by out-of-pocket expenses.

For example, if the defendant causes a car accident and the plaintiff is seriously injured, the plaintiff may sue the defendant for negligence and recover $100,000 for medical bills, $20,000 for lost wages, and $1,000,000 for the impairment of his ability to work and earn a living.

Remedies in Contract

There are nine courses of damage for those suing for breach of contract:

1. Compensatory damages
2. Consequential damages
3. Liquidated damages
4. Rescission
5. Restitution
6. Reformation
7. Specific performance
8. Reliance
9. Expectation interest

Compensatory Damages

In contract cases, compensatory damages are the sum of money it takes to restore the injured party to the economic position it would be in if the contract had been performed. Compensatory damages reimburse the plaintiff for loss. Compensatory damages flow directly from the contract. They are direct damages.

To receive compensatory damages, the injured party must prove the breach of contract caused the damages and that the damages can be quantified with reasonable certainty. For example, merely saying, "The cost to replace my laptop that was destroyed is $1,000," is not sufficient. The court will likely require a purchase receipt or other evidence as proof of its value.

Consequential Damages

Consequential damages occur after the contract is breached. They are awarded when they can be reasonably anticipated. Consequential damages are those that result from the unique circumstances of the injured party. For example, if Sam's Contracting Co. agreed to remodel an apartment complex by June 1 but fails to finish the job until October 1, it is reasonably foreseeable that the apartment complex owner will lose three months rent as a result of the delay. (assuming it can demonstrate it would have tenants) So not only does Sam's breach result in actual damages, it also results in consequential damages consisting of lost revenue for the apartment owner for which Sam's may be liable.

Liquidated Damages

Liquidated damages are awarded when a contract states in advance how much a party must pay if it breaches the contract. It is common for construction contracts to include a liquidated damages clause that penalizes a contractor for each day after the completion date a project remains unfinished.

The court will usually enforce liquidated damages clauses if two conditions hold:

1. At the time of creating the contract, it was very difficult to estimate actual damages.
2. The amount of liquidated damages is reasonable. (If the amount of liquidated damages is determined unreasonable, it may be deemed a penalty and will not be enforced.)

Rescission

When rescission is used, the contract is canceled and both sides are excused from further performance. Any money that has been advanced is returned. Rescission puts the parties where they were before they entered into the contract.

Restitution

Restitution is designed to return to the injured party a benefit it has conferred on the other party, which it would be unjust to leave with that party. It is used when the plaintiff has conferred a benefit on the defendant that requires compensation.

In quasi-contract cases, restitution is used where one side benefits even though the parties never had an enforceable contract. Because it would be unfair to let the party retain the benefit without compensating the other party, the court will require the one who benefited to compensate the party who has provided the benefit.

Restitution is common in fraud, misrepresentation, duress, and mistake cases, and may be used in conjunction with rescission.

Reformation

If a contract is reformed, its terms are changed to reflect what the parties actually intended. Reformation occurs when the court "rewrites" a portion of the contract. This remedy is seldom used but when rewriting the contract can save it, the court may choose to do so.

For example, Sam agrees to sell Sally his 1968 Camaro, but instead of specifying *Camaro* in the contract he says 1968 Corvette. Sam refuses to sell her his 1968 Corvette and Sally sues seeking specific performance. If the court determines that Sam made a mistake, it may "reform" the contract so that it reads 1968 Camaro, as was intended.

Specific Performance

Specific performance is an equitable remedy used when money damages will not help the injured party. In specific performance, the party is ordered to perform the contract as entered into. This remedy is only used in cases involving the sale of land or some other unique asset such as artworks, patents, and trade secrets. Either the seller or buyer may be granted specific performance. Specific performance is not used when the injured party can purchase an identical item with money damages.

Reliance Damages

Money spent on the anticipation that the contract would be performed is considered reliance damages. Reliance occurs when the plaintiff may not be able to demonstrate expectation damages but may still prove that the plaintiff expended money in reliance of the contract.

The reliance interest is intended to put the injured party in the position it would have been in if the parties had never entered into a contract.

Reliance damages are the only type awarded in promissory estoppel cases. In promissory estoppel cases, there has been no bargain (no contract) so there can be no expectation damages for the full benefit of the bargain.

Expectation Interest Damages

An expectation interest is what the injured party reasonably thought it would get from the contract. Expectation interest is intended to put the injured party in the position it would be in if the contract had been performed. Lost profits are considered expectation damages.

Incidental Damages

Incidental damages are the minor costs the injured party suffers when responding to the breach.

UCC Rules

The UCC has specific rules for breach of contracts for the sale of goods.

Seller's Remedies

Under the UCC, the seller may be awarded the difference between the original contract price and the price the seller would have been able to obtain in the open market.

For example, if the buyer breaches a contract to purchase corn from the seller at $2.00 a bushel and the seller was then able to get only $1.50 a bushel by selling the corn on the open market, the seller may sue the intended buyer for $0.50 for each bushel the intended buyer was contracted to purchase.

Buyer's Remedies

Under the UCC, the buyer may obtain the difference between the original contract price and the cover (substitute) price of the goods. The buyer is also entitled to consequential damages if the seller could have reasonably foreseen them.

For example, if the seller breaches the contract by failing to deliver tires and the buyer cannot manufacture and deliver the cars it makes as a result, its lost profit would be a foreseeable consequence of the breach that the seller would be responsible for.

Injunctions

An injunction is a court order that requires a party to refrain from doing something it otherwise would do. The requirements for obtaining an injunction are usually established by statute. For example, an injunction may be issued by the court to stop a city from tearing down a dilapidated building if the property owner demonstrates the statutory requirements necessary to obtain an injunction.

The typical elements necessary to obtain an injunction require a party to show all four things:

1. Potential irreparable injury
2. A likelihood the action will occur if not enjoined
3. There is no other remedy available
4. The court needs to act to prevent the harm

Reparative injunctions are used to undo or reverse harms that have already occurred. For example, if farmer Sam erected a dam on a river as it flowed through his property, which prevented the river from flowing elsewhere, the court may order him to remove the dam so other farmers can access the river's water.

Mandamus

Mandamus is a court order that directs a public official to perform a nondiscretionary official duty. It cannot be used to order a private party.

For example, if the city clerk doesn't like the new law requiring cities to issue marriage licenses to gay couples and he refuses to issue them, a gay couple seeking to obtain a marriage license from him may obtain a court order compelling him to issue the license. The court will order the clerk to do what his job requires.

Mitigation of Damages

Courts will not allow a party who is injured by a breach of contract to recover for damages it could have avoided with a reasonable effort.

A party is expected to mitigate its damages. That means the party must keep damages as low as reasonably possible and must prevent unnecessary loss.

For example, if a tenant breaches a lease and the landlord has another person who wants to rent the apartment, the landlord cannot refuse to relet the apartment and claim the remainder of the unpaid lease money as damages.

Reducing or Increasing Damage Awards

Sometimes a party may appeal a case on the basis that the amount of money damages awarded by the judge or jury is too great or too little.

If the appellate court reduces the amount of damages or compensation on appeal it is called *remittitur*. If the appellate court increases the amount of damages or compensation on appeal it is called *addititur*.

Effect of Third-Party Sources of Compensation

A plaintiff who is injured and receives compensation from a source independent of the defendant may still recover from the defendant for the same loss compensated for by the independent source. This typically refers to insurance payments and provides that although a party has received proceeds from an insurance policy, it is still entitled to recover from the party that was in the wrong.

Attorney Fees

Both tort and contract cases may ask for an award that pays attorney fees, but they are rarely granted. Sometimes a contract may specify that the loser is to pay attorney fees.

Hypothetical Case

Sam's Construction Company has a contract to build a pole barn for Sally's Car Dealership. The contract specifies $1,000,000 in liquidated damages if the barn is not completed by July 1. Due to a late thaw, the barn isn't finished until July 15. Will Sam's company have to pay the $1,000,000 in liquidated damages? Why or why not?

Chapter 24
Insurance Contracts

Introduction

What is insurance? *Insurance* is designed to protect individuals and companies from the uncertainty of events of chance. It is a method of transferring the risk of loss from the individual or business to the insurance company.

There are three types of insurance coverage:

1. Marine and inland
2. Life
3. Fire and casualty

A policy for insurance is a contract. Insurance policies are different from other contracts, and there are separate laws that apply to them.

Contents of Insurance Policies

Typically, an insurance policy will contain nine elements:

1. A description of parties insured
2. The term of policy (its duration)
3. How much each type of coverage costs
4. Endorsements (An endorsement is attached to the policy and modifies or changes the original policy in some way.)
5. Legal description of what is insured
6. Description of the insurance coverage

7. Definitions of terms used
8. Policy exclusions
9. The policy of coverage

Although the legislature mandates certain language that must be included in an insurance policy, there are often ambiguities about the scope of the coverage that result in litigation.

Who Is an Insured?

An insured is the person or company whose loss triggers the insurer's duty to pay the proceeds of the policy. It is almost always the person or company who enters into a contract with the insurer who receives the proceeds in the event of a loss.

Specific Designations

The most common insurance policies cover a person's life or property. It is usually possible to make additions to insurance coverage after the policy is in effect through an endorsement on the policy. An *endorsement* is a written document that is attached to an insurance policy that modifies the policy by changing the coverage provided under the policy. An endorsement can add coverage for parties, or it can add coverage for acts or property that are not covered under the original policy.

Omnibus Clause and Coverage

Insurance liability policies designate at least one insured by name and other insureds by description, usually as classes of people who have some relationship to the named insured. The clause usually defines "insured" as the actual person, spouse, or members of the household. Typically, all included individuals have a specified relationship to the named insured. Each person within each described class is an insured for purposes of the policy's coverage.

Reasonable Belief Clause

This clause excludes coverage for a family member who is operating a motor vehicle without permission of the named insured.

The Loss Payable Clause

This clause refers to the measure of reimbursement a person is entitled to receive when multiple parties share an interest in property. Sometimes the person who owns a life insurance policy is not the person insured. This situation usually arises when a person buys a policy to insure that the debt owed on real property will be paid if one of the purchasers dies before it is paid off. Therefore, the rights of ownership belong to the purchasers, not the insured.

Insurance Policies as Adhesion Contracts

Adhesion contracts are formed when one party has superior bargaining power that it uses to impose its desired terms on the other party. This results in a "take it or leave it" option for the insured. An exclusion of coverage contained in an adhesion contract of insurance must be expressed in words that are plain and clear. An adhesion contract will be strictly construed against the insurer.

Doctrine of Reasonable Expectations

When an insurance contract is ambiguous and subject to two interpretations, and one interpretation is absurd while the other is reasonable, the court will apply the reasonable one.

The reasonable expectations doctrine does not apply unless the contract language is ambiguous. An ambiguous clause is one that is capable of more than one meaning.

Forming an Insurance Contract

The initial insurance contract requires the submission of an application, issuance of binder, investigation by the insurer, and delivery of the policy.

Most insurance agents are considered employees, and most brokers are considered independent contractors. A broker has access to a number of insurers and is actually an agent of the insured.

Duty of the Agent or Broker to the Insured

The insurance agent has a duty to obtain the insurance that the potential insured requests. The agent does not have the duty to offer advice, but if the agent undertakes to offer advice, he or she is then liable for the advice offered.

An agent has a duty to tell the insured what kind of insurance to get if the agent is a specialist in the area, such a duty is imposed by statute, or there is a special relationship between the agent and the potential insured.

Duty of the Agent to the Insurance Company

The duty of the agent to the company is the same as in agency law; meaning the agent must act with due care and act only within the authority of what the principal or the company has authorized. The agent has a duty to act within the authority granted to it and to abide by the company's rules. The agent can be sued by the insurer if the agent orally binds the company to a contract it has not agreed to or if the agent misrepresents a material fact to the insured.

An agent binds the insurance company if two conditions both hold:

1. The agent has either express (actual) or implied (apparent) authority.
2. The facts of the case indicate the agent had authority. The court will look to see if the agent's actions were undertaken with the permission or acquiescence of the insurer (even if the agent acted in excess of their actual authority).

Beneficiaries of Life Insurance Policies

A beneficiary in a life insurance policy is the person who, although not a party to the contract, is entitled to receive the proceeds of the insurance. The two types of recognized life insurance relationships are family and business relationships.

Beneficiary's Rights

Most insurance policies explicitly reserve to the insured the power to change the beneficiary without the designated beneficiary's knowledge or consent. The insured is reserved the power to receive the cash value of the policy, take out loans against the policy, or assign the policy, all without the beneficiary's consent. The beneficiary does not have a vested right and only has an expectancy of receiving proceeds under the insurance policy.

Naming and Designating the Beneficiary

The person who takes out the insurance policy has the right to name and change the beneficiary so long as the beneficiary has an insurable interest in the insured.

Changing the Beneficiary

The insurance policy states how the beneficiary may be changed and when the change becomes effective. Most courts require that the person substantially comply with these provisions rather than comply exactly as the provision specifies.

Creditor or Beneficiary

Most state laws exempt insurance policies from creditor claims. However, the courts will examine five elements:

1. Whether the cash value of proceeds are being claimed as exempt
2. The kind of policy involved
3. The relationship of debtor to policy
4. If debtor is owner or has right to change in beneficiary
5. The relationship of beneficiary to insured

Creditor as Beneficiary

Courts will usually infer that the insured intended to designate the creditor as a beneficiary only to the extent of the debt, although there are some courts that will allow the creditor to keep all of the proceeds.

Covered Risks

Homeowners insurance policies incorporate into one policy several kinds of property coverage: additional living expenses, comprehensive personal liability coverage, property replacement costs, and coverage on the dwelling and adjacent structures.

Auto insurance policies cover many types of liability such as medical payments, uninsured motorist, property damage, and general liability.

Umbrella policies provide liability insurance in excess of that provided by the homeowners and auto policies. This insurance only applies when catastrophic events happen and the insured usually must demonstrate having the maximum coverage with their primary policy before being allowed to purchase umbrella coverage.

Commercial liability coverage provides general insurance coverage to an insured regardless of the nature of the insured's business.

Limitations of Coverage

An insurance policy may, and often does, include explicit limitations, exclusions, or exceptions. These appear in the policy as affirmative grants of coverage or in specific limitations on those grants of coverage. Exclusions and exceptions are areas singled out in the policy where no insurance coverage will be provided.

Termination of Coverage

When an insurance contract has been fully performed, the parties' duties are discharged and the contract terminates. A policy may also terminate on the date of a breach of warranty, a misrepresentation, or the concealment of material information.

Cancellation of Coverage

Insurance coverage can be canceled in four ways:

1. The policy may be rescinded by mutual agreement.
2. An insured fails to pay the premium.
3. The insured may have an explicit right under the policy to cancel it unilaterally.
4. An insurer has the right to cancel the policy unilaterally if not restricted by statute.

Unilateral Cancellation

Usually, the insured can unilaterally cancel the policy at any time, but this right may be abrogated by statute. An insurer always has the right to cancel a policy when there is misrepresentation, concealment, breach of warranty, or premium is not paid.

Statutory Cancellation Procedures

Most state statutes require an insurer to give notice to the insured before effectuating a cancellation. If notice is not given by the insurer, the cancellation is considered void. This is to give the insured both the opportunity and time to obtain other insurance to replace the canceled policy.

Coverage for Intentional Conduct

An insurer will only pay for a loss that is fortuitous—meaning, the loss must be accidental. Insurance policies specifically exclude coverage for intentional acts that result in a covered loss.

Property Insurance

If an insured intentionally causes damage to the insured's own property, the loss will not be covered. The public policy behind this is that allowing damages to be collected on property deliberately damaged by the insured would encourage insureds to destroy their property to collect the insurance money. Also, when an insured intentionally fails to take steps to preserve property after it is damaged, the insured will not be allowed to recover for any additional loss caused thereby.

Personal Insurance, Life, and Accidental Death

Typically, a death due to suicide two years after the policy has been issued excludes coverage. The rationale behind this rule is to prevent a person from purchasing insurance while having the intent to kill oneself for the enrichment of the beneficiaries. In addition, the law views suicide as being inherently nonaccidental.

Determining an Accident

One of the most litigated aspects of insurance policy is determining whether an act is the result of an accident or intentional conduct. This is important because insurance policies do not cover intentional conduct.

An accident is usually considered an unusual event that the insured does not foresee. An example would be an event that happens unexpectedly and without the insured's intent. When determining if the insured's death was accidental the examiner will determine the following:

- Was the death-producing event an accident? (Was the event unforeseen and unexpected from the viewpoint of the insured?)
- If the event was accidental, did the accident cause the death?
- If there are multiple causes of death:
  - Was the accident not too remote?
  - Was the accident the dominant cause of the loss?

Some accidental death provisions require that the insured's death be within a specified number of days of the death-inducing injury. These clauses are increasingly controversial as the ability of the medical profession to prolong life improves.

Disability Insurance

Disability insurance covers the loss of a person's capacity to work. Disability insurance pays an insured person an income when that person is unable to work because of an injury or illness. However, depending on the amount of the policy, it may, or may not pay an amount equal to the income earned while the insured was working.

Occupational Insurance

Occupational disability insurance provides coverage if the insured is disabled from performing the duties of the particular occupation in which the insured is engaged.

General Disability Insurance

General disability insurance policies require that the insured must be unable to pursue an occupation for profit for which he or she is reasonably suited by education, training, or experience.

Health Insurance

Health insurance covers the cost of medical treatment and care when an insured suffers an injury or illness.

Preexisting Conditions

Often times, insurers will exclude from coverage any sickness or illness that existed before the effective date of coverage.

Medically Necessary Services

Medically necessary services means treatment that does not comport with medically accepted medical care protocols and is therefore deemed by the insurer as not medically necessary and is therefore not covered.

Claim Process

To receive insurance proceeds, the insurer typically has to file a claim stating the loss suffered. This process is usually specified in the policy and requires that notice be given to the insurer as soon as possible. However, the insured's noncompliance with the claims processing requirements does not usually allow the insurer an excuse for not performing the duties it has undertaken. The purpose of requiring the insured to give notice of a loss to the insurer is to enable the insurer to investigate the circumstances of the loss before information becomes stale or disappears. It assists in dealing with fraudulent claims and thereby reduces the costs of coverage.

Proof of Loss

The insured must provide some proof of their loss with their claim to give the insurer an adequate opportunity to investigate the loss and to prevent fraud against the insurer.

Substantive Requirements

The insurance policy will specify what proof of loss is required.

Effect of Noncompliance

Generally, noncompliance with the provision requiring proof of loss will only relieve the insurer from providing liability if there was a lack of substantial compliance.

False Statements

Most insurance policies will be considered void if the insured willfully concealed or misrepresented a material fact concerning a loss. However, if the insured makes a mistake, most courts will usually construe it as "false swearing" and the policy will not be considered void.

Disposition of Claims

An insurer must process the claim of an insured in a timely manner. In fact, many insurance contracts provide specific language as to what the time limit is. The time limits cannot be unreasonably short or longer than the time allotted under the statute of limitations.

Insured's Duty to Cooperate with the Insurer

The duty of the insured to cooperate with the insurer may be expressly stated or implied through the insurance contract.

The duty to cooperate does not have to be expressly stated for it to be required. However, a nonbreaching party is not allowed to suspend acting in faith because the other party did not cooperate. It will only be allowed to do so only if the breach of the duty to cooperate is material. In such an instance, the nonbreaching party may be allowed to suspend and ultimately discharge its obligations. Obviously, the cooperation of the insured is necessary because it is the only way that the insurer can obtain the information it needs.

Bad Faith and Breach of Covenant of Fair Dealing

Bad faith is when an insurer denies a claim that is not fairly debatable. An example would be if the insurer fails to pay a claim in a manner that would eliminate the insured's hardship where the insurer is aware of the insured's dire circumstance and has no legitimate reason not to pay the claim.

Duty to Defend

The insurance company has a duty to defend the insured in any lawsuit alleging claims covered under its policy if liability were later established and the insurer would be required to pay damages on behalf of the insured. This duty to defend is based on the allegations in a complaint and is not dependent on their truthfulness.

Duty to Pay Proceeds

Under the contract, the insurer will pay the proceeds of a loss if it is within the coverage provided under the policy. If the insurer wrongfully refuses to make such payments, it may be liable for acting in bad faith.

Measuring the Amount of Loss

The goal of property insurance is to indemnify the insured for the loss covered. Indemnity is to reimburse the insured for the loss sustained and no more. The objective is to put the insured in the position the insured would have been in had the loss not occurred. As such, the insured is not entitled to recover more than the damaged property is worth or more than its decline in value suffered as a result of the damage.

If the insured's loss is partial, they will not be allowed to recover an amount exceeding the policy limits, even if the insured's actual loss were greater. Whatever the limits of policy, the insured will not be allowed to recover more than the insured's interest in the property. In no event can the insured recover more than the value of the property. However, if the insured can show that the damaged boat cannot be restored to as good a condition as it was in before the accident, some courts will allow the insured to recover the difference between the reasonable value of the boat before the accident and the reasonable market value after repair in addition to the cost of repairs.

Co-insurance

Co-insurance is a loss-sharing agreement between the insured and the insurer where the insured bears a portion of the loss based on a percentage of the property's total value not covered by the insurance. The insured is also an insurer along with the underwriter; meaning if the underwritten amount is less than the value of the property, the insured is a co-insurer in the sense that the owner bears a portion of the risk of loss.

Coinsurance requires the insured to pay beyond a deductible before the insurer will provide coverage.

Chapter 25
Agency

Introduction

What is agency? *Agency* is a personal, non-assignable obligation to act on behalf of another that is based on trust and confidence. In agency relationships, the agent is authorized to act on another's behalf in situations involving money, property, specialized knowledge or judgment, and discretion. Agency relationships are often used in commercial transactions, but they may be used for non-commercial purposes as well. Whenever a person or organization seeks to act through the efforts of others, an agency situation may arise. Neither written consent nor compensation is necessary to create an agency relationship.

All agents are fiduciaries—meaning that they have a legal obligation to act in the best interests of their principal. However, not all fiduciaries are agents.

In single agency situations, an agent represents one party to the transaction. In dual agency situations, an agent represents both the principal and the third party in the transaction, with the informed consent of both of them.

Parties to an Agency Relationship

There are three parties in any agency relationship: the principal, the agent, and the third party.

Principal

The principal is the person who delegates the authority.

Agent

The agent is the person who accepts authority and acts on behalf of the principal.

Sometimes a principal may hire an intermediary agent who is given the authority to hire others. The persons hired by the agent are *subagents* of the principal, and the principal may be liable for their actions as well as those of the agent.

Third Party

The third party is the person whom the agent deals with on behalf of the principal—for example, the customer.

Forms of Agency

There are several types of agency. Each is based on the authority that is delegated and the purpose for which the agency relationship is formed.

Universal Agency

Universal agency is the broadest and most general form of agency. It is ongoing in nature, and the agent can bind the principal if authorized to do so.

General Agency

General agency is narrower in scope than universal agency and has a more specific purpose. It can be ongoing in nature, and the agent may bind the principal if authorized to do so.

Special Agency

Special agency is limited in scope and authority to a single act. It is not ongoing, and the agent may bind the principal only if authorized to do so.

Duties and Liability of the Principal

The principal's duties to the agent are to provide information necessary for the agent to do its job, to be available to the agent as needed, to indemnify the agent in certain circumstances, and to pay the agent compensation if the agency is for hire.

A principal is bound by the acts of their agent if the agent has the authority to perform the acts. Specifically, the principal is liable for the contracts entered into by its agent if made with actual, apparent, or inherent agency authority.

If an agent exceeds its authority, the principal must repudiate the act as soon as the principal becomes aware of it or risk the possibility that the court will order that the principal is bound by it. If, however, a principal wrongfully revokes the agency, the agent may sue for damages if the revocation results in a breach of contract.

When determining if an agent was acting within the scope of its authority, the court will examine such factors as whether the act was the kind that the agent was employed to perform and whether it was undertaken, at least in part, by a purpose to serve the principal.

Undisclosed Principal

There are some situations, such as the purchase of land, when the principal does not want its identity revealed to the third party. In these situations, the acts of the agent bind an undisclosed or a partially disclosed principal, if doing so is usual or necessary in such transactions. Sometimes liability attaches even when the agent's acts were forbidden by the principal.

Principal's Liability for Torts

A principal is liable for physical harm caused by the negligent conduct of agents who are acting within the scope of their employment. The doctrine of *respondeat superior,* which is Latin for "let the master answer," is used to impose liability on the principal. Under respondeat superior, the principal is liable for the agent's misconduct even though the principal was not at fault. This may be true even if the principal tried to prevent the agent from engaging in the tortious conduct. An example of this is when the bar owner is held responsible for the actions of his employee who was hired to expel rowdy customers from the bar. Even if the owner tells the employee not to "hurt people," if the employee forcibly removes a customer from the establishment and tosses him onto the pavement where the customer hits his head on the pavement and suffers injury, the owner may still be held liable for the negligence of the employee.

Although a principal may be held liable for the torts of an employee, the principal is usually not liable for the torts of an independent contractor. When determining whether the agent is an employee or an independent contractor, the court will consider these six questions:

1. What amount of control did the principal exercises over the details of the work?
2. Did the principal supply the tools and the place of work?
3. Did the agent work full time for the principal?
4. Is the agent paid for the time or by the number of jobs performed?
5. Do the principal and the agent think they have an employer–employee relationship?
6. Is the principal in business?

Basically, the more control a principal has over an agent, the more likely the agent is to be considered an employee of the principal rather than an independent contractor.

Scope of Employment

Principals are only liable for the torts of their agent/employees that are committed while the employee/agent was acting within the scope of their employment. An agent is usually considered to be acting within the scope of their employment if the agent's actions meet several of these six criteria:

1. The activity is one that agents are usually responsible for.
2. The action took place during hours the agent/employee is generally employed.
3. It is part of the principal's business.
4. The action is similar to one the principal authorized.
5. The principal supplied the tools.
6. It is not an intentional tort.

An act may be determined to be within the scope of employment even if expressly forbidden by the principal if it is of the same general nature as that authorized.

The employer is not liable for the torts committed by agents who are acting outside the scope of their employment unless it can be shown that the principal intended the tortious conduct, the employer was negligent or reckless, or the conduct violated a non-delegable duty of the employer.

Negligent Hiring

Generally, principals are not liable for the physical torts of an independent contractor, but if the principal is shown to have been negligent in the hiring or supervising of the contractor, the principal may be held liable for the contractor's actions. An example is when liability is imposed on stores that failed to check the criminal backgrounds of people they hire as security guards. In some instances, when a security guard with a violent criminal background has assaulted a suspected shoplifter, the store has been found liable to the injured party because the store was determined to have acted negligently by failing to adequately screen the people it hired for security guard positions.

The Agent's Duties to Third Parties

An agent has the duty to act honestly, competently, and fairly when dealing with third parties on behalf of the principal. Often, the third party will be a customer, or potential customer, of the principal. When dealing with third parties, the agent must follow all laws and disclose all relevant information and material conditions of which they are aware.

The Agent's Fiduciary Duties to the Principal

An agent acting on behalf of a principal must act in the best interests of the principal, remain loyal and obedient to the principal, and disclose all relevant information to them. They must also keep confidential any information with which they have been entrusted and provide an accurate accounting of all money and resources that they have been provided. In addition, they must exercise reasonable care and due diligence in all their undertakings.

Methods of Creating Agency

An agency relationship may be created by an express agreement, an implied agreement, by estoppel, or ratification.

Express Agreement

In an express agreement the principal and agent specifically agree to create an agency relationship either orally or in writing. The terms and conditions of the agency relationship are typically specified in detail.

Implied Agreement

It is possible for the court to find an implied agency agreement if the principal and agent appear to have created an agency relationship by words or action.

Agency by Estoppel

If the principal leads a third party to believe a person is the principal's agent through words or conduct, then the courts will not allow the principal to deny the agency relationship.

Agency by Ratification

If the principal accepts an unauthorized act of an agent after the fact, and accepts the benefits of it, the court will rule that the principal has ratified the agent's act and thereby created an agency relationship.

Legal Consequences of the Agency Relationship

Under common law, the principal is responsible for any authorized acts of the agent and any subagents.

Any notice that is given to the agent by a third party is considered to be notice given to the principal. In addition, the duty of confidentiality imposed on the agent is deemed to continue even after the agency relationship ends.

A principal is not bound by the unauthorized assertions of authority by the agent and will not be held liable for them. If the agent disobeys the principal's instructions, he or she will be responsible for any damages that result from the disobedience. For example, if a principal hires an agent to bid up to $1,000 for the principal on a painting at an auction and the agent wins the auction by bidding $2,000 for the painting, the principal will not be obligated to pay $2,000 for the painting (but the agent may be required to).

Even though a principal may be held responsible for an agent's torts, the agent may also be held responsible for them. It is possible for a judgment to be entered against both the principal and the agent.

An agent will be held responsible for any damage that results from its own negligence in the performance of their duties. However, typically, if an agent is employed to secure another agent for the principal, the agent will not be held responsible for the other agent's negligence if due care and diligence were used in securing that agent. An agent will be held responsible for the negligence of his own agent if he hired the person to help him with his agency.

An agent cannot secretly represent both the principal and a third party. They can only do so if both the principal and third party are aware the agent is doing so and they have agreed to it.

An agent employed to buy or sell property on behalf of the principal cannot secretly buy the property and sell it to himself. If it is discovered that he has done so, the transaction can be rescinded.

Estoppel

Under the doctrine of estoppel, the principal may not claim that a person was not his or her agent if the principal knew that others thought the person was acting on his or her behalf and failed to correct the mistaken belief. In such instances, the principal will be prevented (estopped) from denying an agency relationship, and the results of it will be enforced.

Agency Authority

There are three forms of agency that are recognized by courts:

1. Employer/employee or proprietor/independent contractor agency
2. Master/servant agency
3. Principal/agent agency

Every party seeking to enforce or sue based on an agent's acts must demonstrate to the court's satisfaction that the agent was authorized to act on behalf of the principal, master, or employer. To do this, the party may demonstrate the agency relationship was based on apparent or implied authority or that the acts of the agent were ratified.

Apparent Authority

Apparent authority exists when the principal manifests consent to a third party in a way that gives the impression that the principal has authorized the agent to act on the principal's behalf. Courts use the doctrine of apparent authority to protect third parties who have been misled into believing an agent has the authority to bind the principal. Apparent authority may be deduced from words, written documents, and/or the conduct of the principal.

Inherent Authority

Inherent authority is authority that arises solely from the designation by the principal of a kind of agent who ordinarily possesses certain powers. If there is authority that is neither actual nor apparent, then it is inherent. An example of inherent authority is when a real estate agent, who has been authorized to sell a house for the principal, places a "For Sale" sign on the property. The agent does not need to seek special permission from the principal to do this since the action is typically understood to be within the authority given to real estate agents.

Ratification

If someone appears to act on the behalf of another in a transaction with a third party, and the purported agent acted without actual agency authority or power, and estoppel cannot apply, the act is deemed ratified if the principal subsequently affirms it. In such instances, the law holds that a person who accepts the benefits of an unauthorized transaction, or fails to repudiate it, is bound by the act as if he or she had originally authorized it. The person is treated as if he or she ratified the act. Thus, even if an agent acts without authority, the principal can later decide to be bound by the agent and the agent's acts so long as four conditions are met:

1. The agent indicates to the third party that the agent is acting for the principal.
2. The principal knows all the material facts of the transaction.
3. The principal accepts the benefits of the entire transaction.
4. The third party does not withdraw from the contract before the principal ratifies it.

There can be no ratification of the agent's acts if the third party withdraws before the ratification takes place.

Duties and Liability of Agents

Unless otherwise agreed, agents must act solely for the benefit of the principals in all matters connected with their agency. It is also assumed that agents will only undertake actions that are within the bounds of the agency arrangement. An agent is liable to the principal for breach of the duty loyalty, the misappropriation of assets entrusted to the agent's keeping, and a breach of duty of care.

Agent's Liability for Contracts

Agents are not liable for any contract they make on behalf of a fully disclosed principal. Principals are fully disclosed if the third party knows of their existence and their identity.

If a principal is partially disclosed, the wronged third party can recover from either the agent or the principal. A principal is partially disclosed if the third party knew of the principal's existence but not their identity. In the case of a partially disclosed principal, the agent and the principal are jointly and severally liable; meaning the injured party can recover from either or both.

If the principal is undisclosed, the third party can recover from either the principal or the agent. A principal is undisclosed if the third party did not know of the principal's existence. A contract with an undisclosed principal is binding if the agent informs the third party that there is an undisclosed principal. Real estate purchases are often made by undisclosed principals.

If an agent has no authority, the principal is not liable to the third party but the agent is.

Agent's Fiduciary Duty

Agents must account for all profits made in connection with their agency relationship.

Employees, who are agents of a corporation, cannot use proprietary information gained while employed by corporation to their advantage if they take a job with a company that competes with their current employer.

If a person undertakes a gratuitous agency relationship, the person must still act with due care or notify the principal that he or she will be unable to fulfill the agency relationship.

Principal's Remedies for Agent's Breach of Duty

Principals can recover from their agent any damages the agent's breach of duty has caused. If an agent breaches the duty of loyalty, the agent must turn over to the principal the profits earned as a result of the wrongdoing. The principal may also rescind the transaction wrongfully entered into by the agent.

Duties of Principals to Agents

Just as agents have a duty of loyalty to their principal, principals have a duty to cooperate with their agents. Principals cannot unreasonably interfere with their agents' ability to accomplish their task, and the principals must perform their part of the agency contract.

Principals must reimburse agents (indemnify them) for any expense or damages the agents incur while carrying out their responsibilities. The duty to indemnify agents includes tort claims brought by a third party if the principal authorized an agent's behavior and the agent did not know a tort was being committed. The principal must also indemnify the agent for any liability incurred from third parties as a result of entering into a contract on the principal's behalf.

Termination of Agency

If an agent violates his or her duty of loyalty, the agency agreement automatically terminates. A significant change in circumstances may also terminate an agency relationship. If the change is significant enough to undermine the purpose of the agency agreement, then the relationship ends automatically. Sometimes, when the agent's responsibilities become illegal due to a change in the law, the agency relationship terminates. The following list includes eight other reasons for why the agency relationship may be terminated:

1. Completion of the agency objective
2. Lapse of the time specified in the agency agreement
3. Rescission—a mutual agreement of the parties to terminate the relationship
4. Renunciation of authority by the agent
5. Revocation of authority by the principal
6. Destruction or condemnation of the property that is the subject of the agency
7. Death or incapacity of the principal or agent
8. Bankruptcy of the principal

Remedies for Wrongfully Terminating an Agency Relationship

If an agency relationship is wrongfully terminated, the injured party may sue for the reasonable value of the services rendered or any actual damages sustained.

Hypothetical Case

Sam manages the local ski hill for the owner, Mr. Widget. Widget tells Sam that because business is not good, he is to do everything possible not to give refunds or other compensation to customers. Sally and her sister buy a couple lift tickets, and the first run down Sally's sister falls and breaks her leg. Sally accompanies her sister to the hospital. Later, Sally asks Sam to refund her ticket price since she didn't get to ski at all due to taking care of her sister. When Sam refuses to give her a refund, Sally starts yelling so other people in the lodge can hear her. She screams that Sam is a heartless beast and Widget Slopes is the worst ski hill in the country. Sam tries to grab Sally and force her out of the building, but she pulls away and screams that he's assaulted her. By this time, a small crowd has formed. Sam decides he has to get Sally outside fast, so he uses a maneuver from his old military days and twists both her arms behind her back and drags her out. Once outside, he throws her to the ground and tells her to get out and never come back. He leaves her on the ground and walks back into the lodge. A couple months later, Sally sues Sam and Widget Slopes for $1,000,000 in damages she says she suffered at Sam's hands. She claims her shoulders needed surgery, her wrist was broken, and she suffered severe emotional damage due to the humiliation, embarrassment, and degradation he inflicted on her. Can the doctrine of respondeat superior be used to impute liability against Widget Slopes in this case? Why or why not?

Chapter 26
Landowner Duty of Care

Introduction

What is a landowner's duty of care to the people who enter his or her property?

If a person is injured while on someone else's property, the owner, occupant, or tenant responsible for maintaining the property may be liable. If a person suffers an injury due to the negligent maintenance of the property—such as spills on the floor, abandoned appliances, falling shelves, or fallen trees—that person may successfully sue the landlord if it can be demonstrated that the landlord has failed to maintain the common areas of an apartment complex, including pathways and common stairways, while the tenant might be responsible for the tenant's individual unit.

Under common law, a landowner has three defined duties of care to people who enter his or her property. These duties are based on the three legal classifications of people who come onto the landowner's property:

1. Trespassers
2. Licensees
3. Invitees

Trespassers

A trespasser is someone who enters property without the owner's permission. Under common law, a trespasser does not have to be warned of a dangerous condition on the property unless:

- The condition could cause serious injury or death.
- The condition is dangerous and is unlikely to be noticed.
- The trespasser frequently intrudes on the property and a dangerous condition exists.

If any of these circumstances exist, then the law will impose a duty of care on the landlord.

However, if the trespasser is a child, he or she may be protected under the "dangerous instrumentality" rule. Under this rule, if a "dangerous instrumentality" or condition exists on a particular area of property known by the owner to be frequented by children, the owner has a duty to correct or eliminate the danger. Examples of some conditions considered to be dangerous instrumentalities are live electrical wires, old machinery, rotting buildings, and water ponds.

Licensees

A licensee is a visitor who is explicitly or impliedly invited onto the owner or occupant's property for social purposes. For example, a licensee is someone a landowner allows to hunt on his or her property without paying a fee. If, however, the visitor's presence is partly due to business, it becomes more difficult to determine the visitor's status. For example, someone who trips on your porch steps while coming to sell you a lawn service you don't want may be a licensee if you didn't post a sign on your property prohibiting solicitations. But, that person probably isn't a business invitee since the purpose was not to benefit you as much as it was to benefit the solicitor.

Landowners owe a greater duty of care to a licensee than to a trespasser but less than to a business invitee. This is because a licensee enters the property with permission from the landowner but does so for his or her own benefit and not to benefit the landowner.

Therefore, the landowner must repair known dangerous conditions and warn the licensee of hazardous situations, but there is no requirement to warn of all dangerous conditions, nor is there an obligation to keep the property in a reasonably safe condition for them.

Business Invitees

A business invitee is someone who is expressly or impliedly invited onto the property for a business purpose that benefits both the visitor and the owner or occupier. The most common example of a business invitee is someone who goes into a store to buy merchandise. Both the customer and the store benefit from the potential customer's presence. The invitee is not necessarily a visitor to a store but might also be someone who pays to hunt or fish or cut a Christmas tree on someone else's property. Since the invitee enters property at the landowner's invitation and for the landowner's benefit, the invitee is owed the highest duty of care. The invitee must be warned of any dangerous condition and the property must be kept in a reasonably safe condition at all times.

Business invitees who venture outside the area where they are authorized to be, such as a customer who trips over a mop while looking for a bathroom in an area marked "Employees Only," is usually considered an invitee and not a licensee. Similarly, a person who comes into a store or office to visit an employee and not to conduct business is also a licensee. This difference is important because the owner or occupier of property owes a greater duty of care to a business invitee than to a social guest (invitee). For business invitees, the owner or occupier is obligated to regularly inspect the property and make sure it is free of dangerous conditions. However, in the case of licensees, the owner or occupier is required only to fix or warn about known dangers. If, for example, the property owner does not know there is water on the bathroom floor and a guest slips and is injured, the owner may not be liable. However, if business invitees are known to use the bathroom, the property owner has a duty to inspect and make sure the bathroom remains safe.

Hypothetical Case

Susie is the landlord and manager of a six-unit townhouse apartment complex. Jesse has never been to the complex before but comes to visit his friend Sally, who is a tenant in unit #5. As he is walking to her apartment, a laundry rack falls off the balcony of apartment #4, hitting him in the head and causing him a serious brain injury. Can Susie be held liable for Jesse's injury? Why or why not?

Chapter 27
Landlord Tenant Law

Introduction

What is landlord tenant law? *Landlord tenant law* is a combination of property, negligence, and contract law that is built around the unique relationship between property owners and their tenants. Whenever the owner of a freehold estate in land allows another to have temporary, exclusive possession of the property, the owner has created a landlord–tenant relationship. The person with the freehold (owner) is the landlord and the person being given temporary possession of the property is the tenant. The tenant is said to have a *leasehold* in the property the tenant is being allowed to possess. A leasehold may be for a commercial or residential purpose.

Forms of Tenancy

Tenancies, or leaseholds, are nonfreehold estates. The owner of the property leased retains the freehold, and the tenant merely has a possessory interest in the property. There are different forms of tenancy that may be for a specific period of time or at the will of the property owner.

Term of Years

A tenancy with a beginning and end that is fixed from the outset and expires without notice, and which the death of the landlord or tenant does not effect, is a lease for a term of years.

Periodic Tenancy

A tenancy for a fixed period that continues for succeeding periods (month to month) until the landlord or tenant gives notice is a periodic tenancy. A periodic tenancy may arise by express agreement or by implication or operation of law. Under common law, half a year's notice is required to terminate a year-to-year tenancy, and a month's notice is necessary to terminate a month-to-month tenancy.

Tenancy at Will

A tenancy that is terminable at the will of either the landlord or the tenant can arise expressly or by operation of law. Most statutes require a period of notice in order for one party or the other to terminate a tenancy at will. A tenancy at will ends at the death of one of the contracting parties.

Holdover Tenant

A holdover tenant is not a true tenant but is, rather, a tenant who wrongfully stays in possession of the property after the lease has ended. If the tenant remains after the lease expires, he or she effectively becomes a trespasser and the landlord can sue and seek money for the time the tenant wrongfully remained in possession, as well as damages for trespass. If, however, the tenant only wants to stay one more month and the landlord and tenant do not want to enter into a new lease, they may enter into a periodic tenancy.

Abandoned Tenancy

If a tenant intentionally vacates the property and relinquishes it to the landlord before the lease term, then the tenant is deemed to have abandoned the property (and breached the lease agreement). Traditionally, the landlord had no duty to mitigate damages by seeking a new tenant for the premises, but increasingly states are requiring landlords to mitigate their damages by attempting to re-rent abandoned property. If, however, state law does not impose any duty on the landlord to mitigate the damages, then the landlord may make no effort to re-rent the property and can sue the tenant for damages based on the remaining lease term.

The Lease

A lease is both a conveyance and a contract. It gives the tenant the right to possess and use the landlord's property, and it defines the duties between them. The statute of frauds requires that leases for more than one year be in writing to be valid, while leases for less than a year may be based on an oral agreement.

Leases usually contain specific provisions called *covenants* that are promises made by the landlord to do something or refrain from doing something. For example, a covenant may specify who is responsible for maintaining the premises or how the tenant may use the property.

Subleases and Assignments

Sometimes a tenant may wish to vacate the leased premises and turn them over to someone other than the landlord, or the landlord may sell the property to someone else. Generally, when leased property is sold, the new landlord is substituted for the old one and the lease is not affected. However when a tenant turns the property over to someone else, it may result in either a sublease or an assignment of the lease. The way to distinguish between an assignment and a sublease is to consider how much of the tenant's rights are being transferred. Most states hold that an assignment arises when the lessee transfers his entire interest under the lease (right to possession for the duration of the lease term). If the lessee transfers anything less than an entire interest, even one day less, it is considered a sublease and not an assignment.

In most instances, a landlord is allowed to refuse, even arbitrarily so, a tenant's request to assign the lease. However, more and more states are passing laws that require landlords to consent to the assignment of commercial leases if doing so is reasonable under the circumstances.

Tenant Duties

Tenants, like landlords, have legally recognized duties that are usually specified in the lease agreement.

Duty to Pay Rent

The first duty a tenant has is to pay the rent agreed to in the lease. If no rent amount is specifically agreed upon, the law imposes a duty requiring the tenant to pay a reasonable rental value.

Duty Not to Disturb Other Tenants

Most leases provide that the tenant will not substantially interfere with the ability of other tenants to enjoy their premises. If no such provision is included in the lease, courts will typically follow the common law rule that requires tenants to refrain from committing a nuisance upon their fellow tenants. An example of a violation of this duty occurs when the residents of one apartment play the stereo so loud it prevents neighboring apartment dwellers from sleeping at night.

Duty Not to Commit Waste and Duty to Repair

Tenants have an obligation to keep the landlord's premises clean and sanitary and to refrain from any conduct that will deface or damage the landlord's building. In some instances, the tenant's failure to make repairs or to prevent decay and dilapidation of the landlord's property is regarded as permissive "waste," and the tenant may be liable for the damage that results. *Waste* is a legal term that describes the action of improperly or unreasonably using property in a manner that causes damage to it. Waste may occur from an affirmative act or by a failure to take action. An example of waste is when a tenant fails to mow the lawn, paint the house or otherwise fails to maintain the property as required in the lease and the house decreases in value as a result of its neglected condition.

Duty to Surrender the Landlord's Property

Once the lease term expires, the tenant has a duty to vacate the premises and leave it in habitable condition. This means the roof cannot leak, doors and windows cannot be broken, plumbing, electricity, hot and cold running water, and heat must all be in working order.

Tenant Rights and Remedies

Tenants are entitled to stay in possession of the premises for the duration of the lease so long as they pay the required rent and abide by the other terms of the lease agreement. If, however, the landlord breaches the lease, tenants may sue for damages equal to the difference between the value of property with and without the breach. However, traditionally, tenants were required to vacate the property if they claimed the conditions of the property made it uninhabitable.

Damages

Various states compute tenant damages differently. It is important to check the statute that applies when calculating tenant damages. In some states, the court will subtract the fair market value of the property from the rent due under the lease. In other states, the court will order that rent is whatever the fair market value of the property is determined to be. In still others, the rental amount may be reduced from the original amount based on the court's determination of the diminution in value caused by the landlord's conduct.

If the landlord's breach is substantial however, tenants may have to rely on the theory of constructive eviction, in which case they will have to move out but will be relieved of liability for paying future rent and may be entitled to recover damages for the breach. Sometimes relying on this theory can be risky, because if the tenant moves out and the court determines that the conditions did not amount to constructive eviction, the tenant will be considered to have abandoned the property and will be considered to be the party in breach.

Landlord Duties

The landlord who leases property to a tenant also incurs certain legal obligations.

Duty to Deliver Possession

The most obvious duty a landlord has to tenants is to deliver to them the property being leased. Usually this is not a problem, but if the previous tenant refuses to leave, then, obviously the new tenant cannot move in. In this situation, the landlord is typically required to take action to remove the holdover tenant. However, in a minority of states, the landlord is not required to deliver physical possession of the property and it is up to the new tenant to either evict the holdover tenant or begin charging them rent.

Implied Warranty of Habitability

Traditionally, under common law, a landlord conveyed no warranty of any kind and no implied promises were recognized when the tenant acquired possession of the property. It was truly a take-it or leave-it situation for the tenant. However, most states now recognize certain duties on the part of the landlord to the tenant. First among these is the landlord's duty to warrant that the premises leased to the tenant will be habitable for the purpose leased. If the property turns out not to be habitable, then the tenant may abandon the property and be absolved from their obligation to pay rent. In some states, the law may also allow the tenant to continue staying in possession of the uninhabitable premise while continuing to pay rent, and file a lawsuit for damages. Still others may allow a party to obtain injunctive relief that requires the landlord to make necessary repairs to bring the property into a habitable state.

Quiet Enjoyment

Common law recognized a tenant's right to enjoy the leased property free from physical interference by the landlord. This is known as the *covenant of quiet enjoyment*. This covenant was deemed breached if the landlord physically caused the tenant's eviction. If such an eviction occurred, the tenant had the right to terminate the lease and stop paying rent, and the courts would not hold the tenant liable.

Today, this doctrine has been expanded so the law now enforces an implied covenant of quiet enjoyment that recognizes instances of *constructive eviction*. Constructive eviction occurs when the landlord's action, or failure to act, renders the leased premises unsuitable for the tenant's purpose as defined in lease. A tenant's right to sue on this basis may, however, be waived if the tenant remains on the premises and expressly or implicitly accepts the landlord's interference.

Duty to Return Security Deposit

In most lease situations, a tenant is required to pay a security deposit. A security deposit is to be used by the landlord to cover the cost of expenses incurred to repair damage to the premises caused by the tenant. In most states, the law requires a landlord to return the security deposit to the tenant within a specific period of time after the tenant moves out, or else they must notify the tenant of any damage that the security deposit will be used to repair. Several state laws impose statutory damages of two or even three times the amount of the security deposit if a landlord wrongfully refuses to return a tenant's security deposit.

Landlord's Tort Liability

Under the common law rule, a landlord's responsibilities to the tenant were so limited that there were few instances where a landlord could be found liable to the tenant. However, statutory law has increasingly recognized exceptions to this rule.

Liability for Negligent Repair

Under the negligent repair rule, the landlord does not have a duty to repair dangerous conditions that arise after a tenant moves in, but if he or she does so and the repairs are negligently made, the landlord is liable for any personal injury that results from those negligent repairs.

Liability for Common Areas

A landlord is recognized to have a duty of reasonable care to maintain the common areas of building. Common areas are such places as hallways, foyers, and pathways used by all tenants and visitors to a building. If these areas are not maintained by the landlord, their failure to do so may result in liability for injuries caused thereby.

Liability for Latent Defects

A landlord has a duty to disclose (but not fix) known and latently concealed defects that exist at the beginning of a tenancy. If they do so, they have no liability for them.

Liability for Public Use

Where the premises are leased for a public or semi-public purpose, and the landlord knows at time of leasing that a dangerous condition exists, then the landlord can be held liable for any injury sustained by a public patron (not the tenant).

Liability for Premises That Violate Housing Code Standards

Courts often interpret housing code violations as evidence of negligence—or negligence per se.

Hypothetical Case

Keri wants to open a store specializing in the sale of snowmobiles and personal watercraft, and she negotiates a lease with Jason whereby she will rent a 13,000 square foot building he owns on Main Street for this purpose. They enter into a written lease where Keri agrees to pay $10,000 a month rent for three years and Jason will pay all taxes and utilities for the building. After sixteen months, Keri has established a good business, but one day when she and her employees show up to conduct business as usual, they discover there is no running water in the building. Keri discovers that Jason has not been paying the water bills and the utility company has turned off the water. If you are Keri, what action(s) are you going to take, and why?

Chapter 28
Intellectual Property

Introduction

What is intellectual property? *Intellectual property* refers to creations of the mind such as inventions, music, literary and artistic works, symbols, names, images, and designs used in commerce.

Intellectual property is divided into two categories:

1. Industrial property, which includes inventions (patents), trademarks, and industrial designs
2. Copyright, which includes literary and artistic works such as novels, plays and films, musical works, artistic works such as drawings, paintings, photographs and sculptures, and architectural designs

Federal law protects three types of intellectual property:

1. Patent
2. Copyright
3. Trademark

Patent

Patent is a government grant that permits the inventor exclusive use of an invention for twenty years.

During the twenty years no one else may make, use, or sell the invention without the inventor's permission. In exchange, the inventor is required to disclose information about the invention that will allow anyone to duplicate it when the patent expires.

It is important to note that a person cannot patent an idea but only the tangible application of an idea. Thus, even if you think of a great invention, if someone else makes it first and patents it, you have no legal claim against the person who put that idea into tangible form. It is also true that patent protection is not available for scientific principles, mathematical formulas, or laws of nature.

To obtain a United States patent, an invention must meet these criteria:

- *Novel.* A novel product is one that is unique and has not been described in a publication or used before.
- *Nonobvious.* A product is nonobvious if a person of ordinary skill in the particular area could not invent it.
- *Useful.* A useful invention does not have to be commercially valuable but it does have to have some current use.

Provisional Patent Application

If an inventor is reluctant to go through the time and expense necessary to obtain a patent, he or she may file a provisional patent application (PPA). A PPA is a shorter, simpler, and cheaper process that gives inventors the opportunity to show their ideas and products to potential investors without the full expense of a patent application. Provisional patent protection only lasts a year, after which time the inventor must file a regular patent application or lose any patent protection.

International Patent Treaties

Each country has its own patent laws, which are not the same as U.S. patent laws. To provide a form of universal patent protection, the World Intellectual Property Organization (of the United Nations) drafted patent treaties.

The Paris Convention for the Protection of Industrial Properties is one treaty that requires each member country to grant to citizens of other member countries the same patent rights that their own citizens enjoy. Under this Convention, member countries accept and recognize all patent and trademark applications filed with them from member countries as long as they have followed applicable laws. However, there is no standardized patent law, so laws vary greatly by country.

Copyright

Copyright is the ownership of the expression of an idea. It is a form of intellectual property protection provided by federal law to the authors of "original works of authorship." Original works of authorship includes literary, dramatic, musical, artistic, and certain other intellectual works. Copyright protection is available to both published and unpublished works. It is important to note that copyright does not protect the underlying idea or method of operation. So if a person thinks of a great new song but never plays it or writes it down, there is no copyright protection.

Unlike patent, however, the underlying idea of copyrightable material does not have to be novel. Thus, the expression of the same idea by many people may be protected by copyright if the expressions are different. An example of this is when two different film studios produce a movie on the same subject. Although they may both be about the same subject, a giant human-eating monster, each movie is different and each may be copyrighted.

Copyright Allows

Copyright protection allows the protected party to do the following:

- Reproduce the work in copies.
- Prepare derivative works based on the work.
- Perform the work publicly, in the case of literary, musical, dramatic, and choreographic works, pantomimes, and motion pictures and other audiovisual works.

- Display the copyrighted work publicly, in the case of literary, musical, dramatic, and choreographic works, pantomimes, and pictorial, graphic, or sculptural works, including the individual images of a motion picture or other audiovisual work.
- In the case of sound recordings, perform the work publicly by means of a digital audio transmission.

Copyright Does Not Allow

It is illegal for anyone to violate any of the rights provided by copyright law to the owner of copyright. These rights, however, are not unlimited in scope.

NOTE: A copyright violation is not plagiarism. *Plagiarism* **is a term for an academic offense, usually defined by professional or academic bodies. A person cannot be jailed or fined by a state or federal court for plagiarizing someone else's work. They may, however, be subject to punishment by a non-legal body with the ability to enforce its findings. It is not uncommon for reporters to be fired for improperly using someone else's work or for students to be expelled from a university or college for plagiarism.**

Who Can Claim Copyright?

Copyright protection exists from the time the work is created in fixed form. Fixed form may be writing it down, performing it publicly or any other way of physically expressing the work. The copyright in the work of authorship immediately becomes the property of the author who created the work. Only the author, or those deriving their rights through the author, can rightfully claim copyright.

In the case of works made for hire, the employer and not the employee is considered to be the author.

Section 101 of US Copyright law defines a work made for hire as "a work prepared by an employee within the scope of his or her employment; or a work specially ordered as a contribution to a collective work, as a part of a motion picture, as a compilation, as an instructional text, as a test, or if the parties expressly agree in a written instrument signed by them that the work shall be considered a work made for hire." The authors of a joint work are considered co-owners of the copyright in the work, unless there is an agreement to the contrary.

It is important to note that mere ownership of a book, manuscript, painting, CD, or any other copy of a copyrighted property does not give the possessor the copyright or any of the rights that come from owning the copyright. The law provides that transfer of ownership of any material object that embodies a copyrighted work does not convey any rights in the copyright. Thus, if you buy a music CD, you do not have the right to copy, reproduce, or distribute the songs it contains.

What Works Are Protected?

Copyright protects "original works of authorship" that are fixed in a tangible form of expression. The fixation does not have to be directly perceptible, so long as it may be communicated with the aid of a machine or device (i.e., a computer).

Copyrightable works include the following eight categories:

1. Literary works
2. Musical works, including any accompanying words
3. Dramatic works, including any accompanying music
4. Pantomimes and choreographic works
5. Pictorial, graphic, and sculptural works
6. Motion pictures and other audiovisual works

7. Sound recordings
8. Architectural works

The U.S. Copyright Office views these categories broadly. For example, computer programs and most "compilations" may be registered as "literary works," while maps and architectural plans may be registered as "pictorial, graphic, and sculptural works."

What Is Not Protected by Copyright?

Works that have not been fixed in a tangible form of expression—for example, choreographic works that have not been notated or recorded, or improvisational speeches or performances that have not been written or recorded—are not protected by copyright. Similarly, ideas, titles, names, short phrases and slogans, familiar symbols or designs, mere variations of typographic ornamentation, lettering, coloring, or a mere listings of ingredients are not capable of being copyrighted. Works consisting entirely of information that is common property and containing no original authorship—such as standard calendars, height and weight charts, and lists or tables taken from public documents or other common sources—are not copyright protected.

Joint or Collective Works

The authors of a joint work are co-owners of the copyright in the work unless there is an agreement to the contrary. Copyright in each separate contribution to a periodical or other collective work is distinct from the copyright in the collective work as a whole. The author who contributes the work as part of the collection retains the copyright to his or her work.

How to Secure Copyright Protection

The way in which copyright protection is secured is frequently misunderstood. No publication or registration or other action in the Copyright Office is required to secure copyright. Common law copyright protection exists from the moment the work is put into fixed form. To claim protection under federal law, however, requires registration of the work with the federal Copyright Office and there are definite advantages to registering a work with the U.S. Copyright Office.

Advantages to Copyright Registration

Registration may be made at any time within the life of the copyright, and although it is not a requirement for protection, copyright law provides several inducements and advantages to encourage owners to register their work. Among these advantages are the following:

- Registration establishes a public record of the copyright claim.
- Before an infringement suit may be filed in court, registration is necessary for works of U.S. origin.
- If registration occurs before or within five years of publication, it will establish prima facie evidence in court of the validity of the copyright and of the facts stated in the certificate.
- If registration is made within three months after publication of the work or prior to an infringement of the work, statutory damages and attorney's fees will be available to the copyright owner in court actions. Otherwise, only an award of actual damages and profits is available to the copyright owner.
- Registration allows the owner of the copyright to record the registration with U.S. Customs.

Copyright Notice

Use of the copyright notice may be important because it informs the public that the work is protected by copyright, it identifies the copyright owner, and it shows the year of first publication.

Furthermore, if a work is infringed and a proper notice of copyright appears on the published copy or copies to which a defendant in a copyright infringement suit had access, then no weight will be given to such the defendant's claim of innocent infringement (i.e., he/she didn't know the work was copyrighted).

Copyright notice should contain all the following three elements:

1. The symbol © (the letter C in a circle), or the word "Copyright," or the abbreviation "Copr."
2. The year of first publication of the work. The year date may be omitted where a pictorial, graphic, or sculptural work, with accompanying textual matter, if any, is reproduced in or on greeting cards, postcards, stationery, jewelry, dolls, or toys.
3. The name of the owner of copyright in the work, or an abbreviation by which the name can be recognized, or a generally known alternative designation of the owner. For example: © 2009 John Doe.

Copyright Duration

Under the federal statute, works created on or after January 1, 1978, are automatically protected from the moment of their creation, and copyright protection lasts for the author's life plus an additional 70 years after the author's death. In the case of "a joint work prepared by two or more authors who did not work for hire," the copyright protection lasts for 70 years after the last surviving author's death. For works made for hire, and for anonymous and pseudonymous works, the copyright will last 95 years from publication or 120 years from creation, whichever is shorter.

Transfer of Copyright

Copyright is a personal property right, and it is subject to the various state laws and regulations that govern the ownership, inheritance, or transfer of personal property, as well as terms of contracts or conduct of business.

Any part or all of the copyright owner's exclusive rights may be transferred, but the transfer of exclusive rights is not valid unless that transfer is in writing and signed by the owner of the rights. Transfer of a right on a nonexclusive basis does not require a written agreement.

Copyright Infringement

Anyone who uses copyrighted material without permission is violating the Copyright Act.

To prove copyright infringement, a person must prove the work was original, plus two more things:

1. The infringer actually copied the work.
2. The infringer had access to the original work and the two works are substantially similar.

Fair Use

The *fair use* doctrine permits the use of copyrighted works without permission for news, reporting, scholarship, or research (educational purposes). However, a use that decreases revenue (i.e., copying textbooks) by competing with the copyright holder will not be recognized as legitimate under the fair use exception.

The court looks at four factors in determining whether a particular use is fair:

1. The purpose and character of the use, including whether the use is of a commercial nature or is for nonprofit educational purposes
2. The nature of the copyrighted work
3. The amount and substantiality of the portion used in relation to the copyrighted work as a whole
4. The effect of the use on the potential market for or value of the copyrighted work

Contrary to what some people think, there is no specific number of words, lines, or notes that may safely be used without permission. Also, acknowledging the source of the copyrighted material is not a substitute for obtaining permission to use it.

The Digital Millennium Copyright Act

The Digital Millennium Copyright Act (DMCA) amended U.S. copyright law to limit the liability of Internet service providers (ISP) for user information stored on a system or network that the service provider controls.

The DMCA makes it a crime to circumvent anti-piracy measures built into most commercial software and outlaws the manufacture, sale, or distribution of code-cracking devices used to illegally copy software.

The DMCA does permit the cracking of copyright protection devices to conduct encryption research, assess product interoperability, and to test computer security systems. It also provides exemptions from anti-circumvention provisions for nonprofit libraries, archives, and educational institutions, under certain circumstances.

In general, the DMCA limits ISPs from copyright infringement liability for simply transmitting information over the Internet. ISPs, however, are expected to remove material from users' Web sites that appears to constitute copyright infringement.

The DMCA limits the liability of nonprofit institutions of higher education when they serve as online service providers and, under certain circumstances, for copyright infringement by faculty or graduate students.

Copyright Treaties

The Berne Convention requires member countries to provide automatic copyright protection to any work created in another member country. The protection expires fifty years after the death of the author.

Trademark

A trademark is any word, phrase, symbol, design, sound, smell, color, product configuration, or group of letters or numbers that is adopted and used by a company to identify its products or services and distinguish them from products and services made, sold, or provided by others. Typically, a trademark is used to identify goods. Examples of trademarks are the Apple Inc. logo, McDonald's golden arches "M," the NBC peacock and the mascot of athletic teams.

The primary purpose of trademarks is to prevent consumers from becoming confused about the source or origin of a product or service. Trademarks tell consumers who made the product or who provides the service. As consumers become familiar with particular marks, and the goods or services they represent, trademarks can acquire a secondary meaning as indicators of quality. They can help consumers decide whether a product or service is a good one to buy.

A service mark is another type of mark. Service marks indicate the source or origin of services, as opposed to goods. Kinko's photocopying, Blockbuster Video, and Servicemaster Cleaners are companies that use service marks. For all practical purposes, trademarks and service marks are subject to the same rules of validity, use, protection, and infringement.

Trade names are not always trademarks although they can be. A trade name is a word, name, term, symbol, or combination of these, used to identify a business and its goodwill. Whereas, a trademark identifies the goods or services of a company, a trade name identifies the company itself. However, it is possible for trade names to also function as trademarks. Many companies use all or part of their business names as trademarks for their products. When a trade name is used by a company in this dual fashion, it becomes even more important that it prevent competing companies from using a similar trade name or trademark.

Since trademarks are commercial source indicators, they do not expire. The longer a trademark is used, the more valuable it becomes. Trademarks are acquired through adoption and use with trademark rights arising automatically.

Registering Trademarks

Just as with registering a copyright, there are definite advantages to registering a trademark with the U.S. Patent and Trademark Office (PTO). Marks registered with the PTO enjoy stronger and geographically broader protection. Registered trademarks are indicated by the ® symbol.

An owner protects its trademark rights through registration, maintenance, watching, and enforcement. Nothing that closely resembles an owner's mark should be permitted. In no case does a junior user's mark need to be identical for infringement. Infringement only requires likely consumer confusion.

Trademark Searches

Trademark searches are critical to avoiding legal problems and keeping and maintaining a good reputation. To use "Microsoft" without learning whether that name is already used by another on similar goods is unwise and may result in costly litigation.

Initial trademark searches can be done on the Internet, using one or more search engines. Trademarks should also be checked against state and federal registers. It is also important to look for possible non–trademark users and users in remote markets.

Domain Name Issues

A domain name is a unique name that identifies an Internet site without having to know the true numerical address (e.g., www.nmu.edu).

If a domain name has the potential of confusing the public into thinking the trademark holder is some-how affiliated with another's Web site, product or company, the trademark holder may bring an infringement claim against the person or company causing the deception. For example, if your domain name is applegear. com, people might assume it is affiliated with Apple Inc. They may buy something from your Web site thinking the product is made by or endorsed by Apple when it is not. This would entitle Apple Inc. to bring a trademark infringement lawsuit against you.

Personal names can be used as domain names, and they may be trademarked. This is common for famous athletes and movie stars, and they have filed trademark infringement lawsuits to obtain ownership of their personal domain names.

The use and abuse of domain names became a serious problem as the Internet grew.

It became quite common for people to register domain names that they didn't want or intend to use but knew others would. These *cybersquatters* would then offer to sell the domain names to the corporations or individuals who wanted them at hugely inflated prices. Registering a domain names solely for the purpose of making a lot of money from them, with no intent to use them, is called *cybersquatting*. This became such a problem that Congress passed a federal statute to address it.

The Anticybersquatting Protection Act (ACPA)

The Anticybersquatting Protection Act (ACPA) provides a federal remedy for cybersquatting. It applies to situations in which a person has a bad faith intent to profit from a trademark, including a personal name, which is a protected trademark.

A person violates the ACPA by registering, trafficking in, or using a domain name that:

1. Is identical or confusingly similar to a distinctive mark.
2. Is identical or confusingly similar or dilutes a famous mark.

The ACPA allows the court to order the cancellation of the domain name or the transfer of it to the owner of the trademark, whether the registration of the domain name occurred before or after the enactment of ACPA. It also provides for damages for the registration of domain names that occur after the enactment of the ACPA.

The ACPA permits a plaintiff to seek statutory damages or actual damages and lost profits.

Hypothetical Case

Sam works for Mega Works Inc. as a software engineer. He signed an employment agreement that states that any software programs he designs in the course of his employment are the property of Mega Works. Sam designs a program that creates 3-D images from traditional animations. The company markets this program at great profit. While at home on weekends, Sam takes the same technology he used to design the animation translation program and designs a program that creates 3-D pictures from architect renderings. He patents this program in his name and sells it at great profit. Mega Works learns of this and sues Sam, claiming it is entitled to the patent and profits from his architect program. What facts and law support Mega Works' cause of action, and what facts and law support Sam's defense?

Chapter 29
Estate Planning

Introduction

What is estate planning? *Estate planning* is the process of preparing for the distribution of one's estate at death by using a will, trusts, gifts, power of attorney, and other legal means.

An estate is the total property, real and personal, owned by an individual prior to distribution through a trust or will. It may consist of both real property, which is real estate, and personal property, which includes everything else such as cars, household items, and bank accounts. Estate planning distributes this property to the individual's heirs or others.

The process of estate planning occurs when individuals arrange the transfer of their assets in anticipation of death. An estate plan's purpose is to preserve the maximum amount of wealth possible for the intended beneficiaries, while also providing financial flexibility for the individual prior to their death. A major concern for drafters of estate plans is federal and state tax laws.

It is the law of trusts and estates that governs the management of personal affairs and the disposition of an individual's property in anticipation of incapacity or death. This law is also used to carry out the wishes of philanthropic bequests or gifts through the creation, maintenance, and supervision of charitable trusts.

Wills and trusts are common ways in which individuals dispose of their wealth. Trusts, unlike wills, have the benefit of avoiding probate, a lengthy and costly legal process that oversees the transfer of the decedent's assets. Sometimes, however, it is better to make inter vivos gifts (gifts made while the donor is alive) in order to minimize taxes. The federal gift tax law exempts a certain amount of lifetime gifts.

When individuals die without a will, state law determines the distribution of their property. These probate laws vary from state to state, but typically, the distribution is to an individual's spouse and children, or, if there are none, to other family members. A state's probate distribution system usually provides protections for certain beneficiaries, such as the decedent's spouse and minor children. A will, however, gives an individual the power to alter the state's default system and distribute their assets in the way they desire.

Trusts

During the 1500s, English landowners developed a system of conveying the legal title of their land to third parties while retaining the benefits of owning the land. They developed this system because if they were not the legal "owners" of the land—and wealth was primarily measured by the amount of land people owned—the property was immune from creditors and they were relieved of certain feudal obligations. Today, wealth is held in many forms beside land, such as stocks, bonds, and bank accounts, but the practice of placing property ownership in the hands of third parties for the benefit of another is still used. Today it is called a *trust*.

A trust is a right in either real or personal property, which is held in a fiduciary relationship by one party for the benefit of another. The trustee is the one who holds title to the trust property, and the beneficiary is the person who receives the benefits of the trust and its assets.

The trustee has legal ownership of the property that has been transferred to him or her (or "it" if the trustee is a bank) by the person establishing the trust. The person establishing the trust is called the grantor, settlor, or trustor.

The trust property is known as the trust *principal*, or *corpus* and it and its assets are invested and managed for the benefit of the beneficiaries. Sometimes the grantor may also serve as the trustee and beneficiary. Generally, however, if the grantor is the trustee, the grantor cannot be the only beneficiary.

Trust Variations

As a fiduciary, the trustee must properly manage the entrusted property and make sure that it is used only in the manner, and for the purposes, established by the grantor in the trust document.

Trusts can be *living*, meaning they are established during the grantor's lifetime, or they can be *testamentary*, meaning they are established in a person's will.

A living trust can be revocable, which means it may be terminated or modified at any time by the grantor for any reason. Living trusts are often used to avoid probate, reduce estate taxes, or set up long-term property management.

A significant advantage of living trusts is that property in the trust does not have to go through probate court when the grantor dies. Probate is the court-imposed process of paying the debts of the estate and distributing the remaining estate property to the people who inherit it.

A trust may also be irrevocable. A testamentary trust, which is established by the deceased in the will, is an irrevocable trust. Grantors may change their wills, including any testamentary trust created by it, at any time before their death. In an irrevocable trust, however, grantors can never change or terminate the trust or withdraw assets, even in an emergency.

When establishing a trust, all assets must be formally transferred to the trustee, and trust documents must use this title when indicating ownership. For example, any real estate deeds and financial accounts put into the trust must be re-titled to show they are owned by the trust. Financial institutions also require authorization, in the form of the trust document, before they will accept instructions from a trustee.

Testamentary trusts require that the will be probated. This can be a significant disadvantage over a living trust.

Wills

A will provides for the distribution of property owned by an individual at the time of his or her death. A will cannot dispose of assets that is not part of the probate estate—such as joint property, life insurance, retirement plans, and employee death benefits—unless they are payable to the estate.

Wills can be used to achieve a wide range of family and tax objectives. A will that provides for the outright distribution of assets is characterized as a simple will. If the will establishes one or more trusts, it is called a *testamentary trust will*. The purpose of the trust arrangement, as opposed to outright distribution, is to minimize taxes, ensure that certain property continues to be managed, and to provide creditor protection for the surviving family members.

Other important objectives that may be accomplished by a will are designating a guardian for minor children or providing for a stepchild, elderly parent, or other individual upon one's death.

Estate and Gift Tax

One of the oldest and still most common forms of taxation is the taxation of property held by an individual at the time of their death. This tax is called an *estate tax,* which is a tax levied on the estate before any its property is transferred. An estate tax is charged on the decedent's entire estate, regardless of how it is disbursed.

Another form of death tax is an inheritance tax, which is a tax levied on individuals receiving property from the estate.

Taxes imposed on death provide an incentive for some people to transfer their assets before their death.

Gift tax laws are taxes designed to prevent complete tax avoidance by people transferring their property prior to death. The federal estate tax is integrated with the federal gift tax so that large estates cannot avoid taxation by a lifetime of giving. Many states also have their own estate taxes.

Living Wills

A living will informs others of the kind of medical treatment individuals wish to receive, or not receive, when they are incapacitated and cannot speak for themselves. A living will is a written document that states how a person wants to be treated in certain medical situations. A person may use it to inform family and members of the medical community whether they wish to be given life-sustaining treatments if they become terminally ill or injured.

In addition to terminal illness or injury situations, most states permit individuals to express preferences as to the use of life-sustaining equipment and/or feeding tubes for medical conditions that leave them permanently unconscious and without detectable brain activity.

Living wills apply in situations where the decision to use certain medical treatments may determine whether a person lives or dies. They are not used in situations that do not affect continued life, such as routine medical treatment or non–life-threatening medical conditions. In all states, it is a medical professional who makes the determination of whether someone is in a medical condition in which the living will is invoked.

Power of Attorney

A power of attorney gives one or more persons the power to act on an individual's behalf in legal and/or financial matters. Although it can be used for many purposes, it is often an important part of estate planning. The power of attorney may be limited to a particular transaction, such as selling real estate, or it may be very broad in its application by empowering another to act on their behalf in a wide variety of situations.

A power of attorney may take effect immediately or only upon the occurrence of a future event, such as a person's inability to act for him or herself. The latter is referred to as a *springing* power of attorney.

A power of attorney may give temporary or permanent authority to act on an individual's behalf. Although it may be revoked, most states require written notice of revocation to the person named as having the power of attorney.

The person who is given the power of attorney to act on someone's behalf is referred to as the agent or attorney-in-fact. The agent can take any action permitted in the power of attorney document. Typically, the agent must present the power of attorney document to invoke the power. For example, if you are selling a piece of real estate in a place you do not live and you give a Realtor power of attorney to sell it, the bank or mortgagor will require that the power of attorney document be presented before the real estate agent will be recognized as having the authority to sign the deed and title it over to someone else. This is also true when selling stocks or opening and closing bank accounts. However, an agent usually does not need to present the power of attorney when signing checks for the grantor.

The use of a power of attorney to designate someone to manage one's personal or business affairs may eliminate the need for the court to appoint a guardian to act for the person. People appointed by the court to act on behalf of incapacitated persons are called guardians or conservators. The power of attorney allows people to choose for themselves who will act on their behalf if they are incapacitated and to define their authority, instead of leaving that decision up to the court.

In addition to managing a person's day-to-day financial affairs, the power of attorney may take steps to implement the grantor's estate plan. Although an agent cannot revise a person's will, some jurisdictions permit someone with a power of attorney to create or amend trusts during the grantor's lifetime or to transfer trust assets.

A person with power of attorney may also make gifts on behalf of the grantor, so long as that person follows the guidelines set forth in the power of attorney document.

Since a power of attorney is determined by the law of the state in which a person resides at the time it is signed, consulting that law is required to determine exactly what is allowed.

Hypothetical Case

Jake remarried at the age of forty, and his second wife, Sandy, had two young children at the time he married her. Jake and his stepchildren grew very close during the next twelve years, especially since Jake had no children of his own. When Jake was diagnosed with cancer, he decided he needed to do something to make sure Sandy and her children were taken care of if he didn't survive long. If Jake asks you what he should do, how will you advise him, and why?

Chapter 30
Employment Law

Introduction

What is employment law? *Employment law* governs the relationship between the employer and employee. It controls the nature and degree of the employer's control over employees and how their work is performed. It also encompasses the right of employees to constitutional and statutory protections and benefits.

Until recent times, there was little in the law that recognized rights of employees, as opposed to those of employers. However, with the advent of the Industrial Revolution and the institution of large, and sometimes unsafe, working environments, there has been a shift in how the law deals with the employer/employee relationship. Today, most employer/employee aspects are governed by statute. One of the first statutes to address workers' rights was the National Labor Relations Act (NLRA), which was passed in response to several instances of anti-union violence. This law prohibits employers from penalizing workers who form unions and requires employers to bargain with unions in good faith.

Today, many businesses feel they are overly burdened with laws and regulations that govern their relationship with employees. This is an area where there are numerous federal as well as state laws that businesses must be aware of and abide by.

Employer Rights and Obligations

An employer has a right to expect its employees to be punctual and honest, and to perform all reasonable and legal work-related requests made of them. In exchange, an employer is expected to provide a safe and healthy workplace, pay and keep records of the wages it pays its employees, and avoid discriminatory practices.

When asked, most employers state that the most difficult aspect of their task in dealing with employees is complying with state and federal laws that govern so many aspects of the employer/employee relationship. This is truly a formidable task, which is why so many companies hire someone whose entire job consists of monitoring and ensuring compliance with state and federal laws and regulations. This job is made even more difficult by the fact that employment-related laws and regulations are continually being created, amended, revised, and repealed.

Federal Statutes Applicable to Employers

There are many laws and regulations that impact the way employers treat their employees. There are laws that govern employment taxes, the rights of workers to take unpaid leave to help an ailing family member, and laws that protect workers who report the illegal conduct of their employer. The laws of the state in which the business operates should always be consulted, but some of the federal statutes that employers must remain knowledgeable about are listed here:

ADA—Americans with Disabilities Act, prohibits public and private employers, employment agencies and labor unions from discriminating against qualified individuals with disabilities in job hiring, firing, advancement, compensation, job training, and other aspects of employment. The ADA covers employers with fifteen or more employees.

ADEA—Age Discrimination in Employment Act, prohibits employers from firing or refusing to hire people aged forty or older due solely to their age. The ADEA applies to employers with twenty or more employees, including state and local governments.

COBRA—Consolidated Omnibus Budget Reconciliation Act, gives workers and their families who lose their health care benefits the right to continue their group health plan for a limited period when they lose their job or in other specified circumstances.

FLSA—Federal Labor Standards Act, establishes minimum wage, overtime pay, recordkeeping, and youth employment standards that affects employees in the private sector as well as those in federal, state, and local governments.

FMLA—Family Medical Leave Act, provides up to twelve weeks of job protected leave and benefits to employees seeking time off work for certain family and medical reasons. It applies to all public and private companies with fifty or more employees.

HIPAA—Health Insurance Portability and Accountability Act, provides federal protection for the privacy of personal health information. It pertains to information created or received by a health care provider, employer, life insurer, school or university, or other health information clearinghouse. It requires patients to give their consent before information about their health condition is released to third parties.

OSHA—Occupational Health and Safety Act, established the Occupational Health and Safety Administration that governs workplace safety and health in both the public and private sectors. Among other things, it is designed to protect workers from such hazards as exposure to toxic chemicals, unsanitary conditions, excessive noise levels, and mechanical equipment dangers.

Title VII of the Civil Rights Act prohibits an employer from discriminating against employees on the basis of race, color, religion, sex, or national origin. It applies to employers who employ fifteen or more employees for more than nineteen weeks in the current or preceding calendar year.

WPA—Whistleblower Protection Act, protects federal government employees who disclose information of wrongdoing or illegal conduct committed by other government employees from retaliation or discharge. Many states have their own version of the Whistleblower Act.

Employment Security

Whereas most employers are concerned with abiding by numerous state and federal laws that govern their relationship with employees, often the most important concern to an employee is the knowledge that they will continue to have a job as long as they perform their job duties as required. Employees want to be secure that if they meet their quota of producing three hundred gizmos per day they will not be fired because their employer learns they are married to a person of a different race. Discrimination can take many forms, and not all of it is illegal. For example, blind people cannot perform the duties of an air traffic controller or a school bus driver, so it is not illegal to discriminate against them for these jobs on this basis. A person's expectation of continued employment, however, typically depends on whether the person is an employee who serves at the will of the employer or if they have a legally recognized employment contract.

At-Will Employment

Individuals are *at-will employees* if their employer can fire them at any time and for any reason. There is no federal statute that prevents states from allowing employers to adopt at-will employment practices, and almost all states allow such. Despite this, most states also recognize four public policy exceptions to this practice:

1. An employee may not be fired for refusing to perform an illegal act.
2. An employee may not be fired for exercising a statutory right (e.g., filing for worker's compensation).
3. An employee may not be fired for fulfilling a statutory obligation (e.g., responding to a summons for jury duty).
4. An employee may not be fired for reporting illegal conduct of the employer.

Employment by Contract

If someone is not an employee who serves at the pleasure of their employer (i.e. an at-will employee), the person's employment status is typically governed by a written employment contract. The terms of the employment contract will dictate the duration of employment, the compensation, benefits, and other employee/employer expectations. If an employee is a member of a union, the union contract may be the contract that governs employment rights and duties.

In some instances, courts have ruled that an employee is protected from termination by an implied contract of employment. In these instances, the terms in an employment application, employee handbook, employer policies, and procedures manual or verbal representations by management may be used by the court to find an implied employment contract. Because of this, employers will try to protect themselves from possible claims of an implied employment contract by requiring that employees sign a form acknowledging that there is nothing in the job application, policy manual, handbook, or other document that constitutes a contract of employment. They use such a form to ensure that employees specifically acknowledge that they are at-will employees who may be terminated at any time for any reason or for no reason at all, with or without advance notice.

Wrongful Discharge

An employer is entitled to dismiss employees pursuant to the terms of their employment contract or, if there is no contract and the person is an employee at-will, for any reason at all. In those instances where a person's employment is terminated without just cause, however, it may give rise to a lawsuit for wrongful discharge or wrongful termination. It is considered a violation of public policy in many states to wrongfully discharge an employee, even in some instances where the employee did not have an employment contract. As stated previously, it may be a violation of public policy that justifies a wrongful discharge suit for an employer to fire an employee for refusing to commit unlawful acts; for exercising a statutory right; for fulfilling a public obligation (such as serving on a jury); or for reporting the wrong-doings or illegal acts of their employer.

Unlawful Discrimination in Employment

In addition to concerns about employment security, many employees fear an employer may illegally discriminate against them. Besides constitutional protections against unreasonable discrimination, there are also federal and state laws that are designed to prevent discriminatory practices by employers. Some of these are discussed in this section.

Title VII

Under Title VII of the Civil Rights Act, an employer is prohibited from discriminating against employees on the basis of race, color, religion, sex, or national origin. However, this prohibition of employment discrimination does not prevent employers from discriminating on the basis of religion, sex, or national origin (but not on race) where religion, sex, or national origin is a bona fide occupational qualification that is reasonable or necessary for performing a particular job. If the employer can demonstrate that discrimination is appropriate, it may be allowed to engage in the conduct under the bona fide occupational qualifications exception. To successfully argue this exception an employer must prove three things:

1. There is a direct relationship between sex and the ability to perform the duties of the job.
2. The reason for the discrimination relates to the "essence" or "central mission of the employer's business."
3. There is no less-restrictive or reasonable alternative.

It should be noted that although this exception may be used, courts scrutinize it very closely and are willing to apply it in very few cases. An employer or customer's preference for an individual of a particular religion or race is not sufficient to establish a bona fide occupational qualification under Title VII.

The Equal Employment Opportunity Commission

The Equal Employment Opportunity Commission (EEOC) as well as some state fair employment practices agencies (FEPAs) are tasked with enforcing Title VII provisions. The EEOC and state FEPAs investigate, mediate, and sometimes file lawsuits on behalf of employees who have been unlawfully discriminated against. However, although Title VII allows individuals to file private lawsuits for violations of the Civil Rights Act, they must first file a discrimination complaint with the EEOC within 180 days of learning of the discrimination. If they fail to file a complaint with the EEOC as required, they may lose their right to file a lawsuit.

Pregnancy Discrimination

Title VII also prohibits differential treatment of women who are pregnant, unless not being pregnant is a bona fide occupational qualification. There is also a Pregnancy Discrimination Act that prohibits discrimination on the basis of pregnancy and treats such as a form of sex discrimination. Under this statute, women who are pregnant or affected by childbirth must be treated the same as all other similarly situated employees with respect to their ability or inability to work.

Age Discrimination

The Age Discrimination in Employment Act (ADEA) protects people forty or older from employment discrimination based on age. Its protections apply to both employees and job applicants. Under this statute, it is unlawful to discriminate against a person because of his or her age concerning any term, condition, or privilege of employment, including hiring, firing, promotion, layoff, compensation, benefits, job assignments, and training. The statute also makes it unlawful to retaliate against a person for opposing employment practices that discriminate based on age or for filing an age discrimination charge, testifying, or participating in any way in an investigation or litigation under the ADEA.

Just as in other employment discrimination cases, proving age discrimination as the reason behind a failure to obtain or retain a position may be extremely difficult. There is no specific test for determining age discrimination, and most cases are factually dependent.

Disability Discrimination

The Americans with Disabilities Act (ADA) makes it unlawful for employers to discriminate against employees or potential employees who are qualified for a job but have a disability. It also outlaws discrimination against individuals with disabilities in state and local government services, public accommodations, transportation, and telecommunications. This law is enforced by the U.S. Equal Employment Opportunity Commission (EEOC) and state and local civil rights agencies that work with the Commission.

Any employer practices that discriminate against an employee in recruitment, pay, hiring, firing, promotion, job assignments, training, leave, lay-offs, benefits, and all other employment-related activities because of a disability are prohibited under this act.

Changes made to the ADA that went into effect in 2009 contained important revisions to the definition of *disability* that rejected the holdings in several Supreme Court decisions and portions of EEOC's ADA regulations. Although it retains the ADA's basic definition of *disability* as an impairment that substantially limits one or more major life activities, a record of such an impairment, or being regarded as having such an impairment, the revised ADA changes the way that these statutory terms are to be interpreted in several significant ways. Basically, the ADA now expands the definition of "major life activities" by including two non-exhaustive lists. The first includes many activities (such as walking) that the EEOC has recognized, as well as activities that EEOC has not specifically recognized (such as reading, bending, and communicating). The second list includes major bodily functions (such as functions of the immune system, normal cell growth, digestive, bowel, bladder, neurological, brain, respiratory, circulatory, endocrine, and reproductive functions).

The 2008–2009 ADA amendment also clarifies that an impairment that is episodic or in remission is a disability if it would substantially limit a major life activity when the condition is active. It also emphasizes that the definition of *disability* should be interpreted broadly.

Sexual Harassment

Discrimination on the basis of a person's gender has been defined by statute to include sexual harassment, which means unwelcomed sexual advances, requests for sexual favors, or other verbal or physical conduct or communication of a sexual nature. Such conduct may be where sex is made a term or condition, either explicitly or implicitly, to obtain employment or employment advancement; where submission to or rejection of the conduct is used as a factor in decisions affecting an individual's employment; or where the conduct or communication has the purpose or effect of substantially interfering with an individual's employment or it creates an intimidating, hostile, or offensive employment environment.

Quid Pro Quo

There are two types of sexual harassment cases. The most common and easily recognized form of sexual harassment is the *quid pro quo* situation. *Quid pro quo* is a Latin phrase that means, "You do something for me and I'll do something for you." In a quid pro quo sexual harassment case, a person claims that because he or she rejected a sexual advance by a person he or she worked with, the person's employment situation suffered tangible harm, such as their failure to be promoted, being fired, or being given less attractive job duties. To demonstrate tangible harm, employees must be able to show they were given extra work or an inappropriate job assignment.

If a quid pro quo situation resulted in tangible harm to the victim employee, an employer may be held vicariously liable for the sexual harassment perpetrated by one of its employees against the other.

Hostile Work Environment

The second form of sexual harassment occurs when an employer creates a hostile work environment for one or more of its employees. A successful hostile work environment claim must demonstrate harassing conduct motivated by gender discrimination that is sufficiently severe or pervasive so as to make the victim's work environment a hostile place. In these claims, no tangible employment harm needs to be shown. It is sufficient if the court finds that a reasonable person would conclude that the environment created by the employer is hostile and abusive under the totality of circumstances. Factors such as the frequency and severity of conduct will be considered, as well as whether the conduct unreasonably interfered with the employee's work. The court may also examine the effect of the conduct on the employee's psychological well-being in determining whether the environment was abusive to the point of creating a hostile work environment.

An employer may successfully defend itself in a sexual harassment suit by demonstrating that it acted with reasonable care to prevent and promptly correct any sexual harassment behavior and/or if it can demonstrate that the alleged victim unreasonably failed to take advantage of any corrective or preventive opportunities offered by the employer. Thus, if an employee is aware of the company's policy against sexual harassment and its complaint process for addressing such problems but fails to use the process and goes directly to court instead, the court may dismiss the case.

Courts have increasingly recognized same-gender sexual harassment claims when it can be shown that the hostile work environment was motivated by a person's sexual orientation or that tangible employment damage occurred because the victim rejected a homosexual advance.

Privacy Protections

Although many employees believe they should be able to use their employer's computer to surf the Internet during their lunch break or to write and store personal e-mail on it, the law does not recognize such a right. The company's computer is recognized to be the employer's property, and therefore the employer is entitled to determine how the employee is to use that property. Most courts do not recognize employees' right to privacy in the workplace when they are using company property or resources.

Electronic Monitoring in the Workplace

Most courts also permit employers to use electronic means to monitor the conduct and work performance of their employees. As a result, it is not uncommon for employers to use software programs that record an employee's Internet activity, e-mail transmissions, and each keystroke they type.

Alcohol and Drug Testing

In most states, private employers are free to use drug-testing programs as a condition of employment or continued employment. However, some state and federal courts have ruled that drug-testing programs in public workplaces are unconstitutional if they are not based on some kind of individualized suspicion. In these cases, the employee must have engaged in some conduct or exhibited some behavior that warrants suspecting they were impaired by drugs or alcohol while on the job.

Off-Duty Conduct

Typically, most jurisdiction hold that what employees do after work is their own business, as long as their conduct is not illegal or of an immoral nature that portrays their employer in a bad light. There are some jobs or employment contracts where the employer makes the employees' exemplary personal conduct a condition of continued employment. An example of this is a company that hires a professional athlete to endorse its products or act as its spokesperson.

Workers Compensation

Workers compensation laws are state laws that provide payment to employees for injuries they incur at, or during, work. If employees' injury are compensated by workers compensation, they are not allowed to sue their employer for negligence in causing their injury. The rationale behind workers compensation laws is that although the compensation the employee receives may be less than what the employee could get through a lawsuit, it is a sum certain, and the employee may receive it a lot quicker. Conversely, an employer who pays into the workers compensation fund is protected from potentially catastrophic legal judgments from negligence-based employee lawsuits.

Hypothetical Case

Regis works as a receptionist at Gizmo Co., which is one of the country's largest suppliers of widgets. He has worked there ten years for the same boss, but when she retires and the new boss, Mr. Snidely, takes over, there are instant problems. Snidely began by commentating to co-workers that Regis was "a fag" and that no man should be allowed to keep a job who wears an earring to work. Whenever Regis would tell Snidely that someone stopped by to see him, he would say things like, "Oh God, I hope they don't think I hired you." Finally, when Regis was the only person in the department who Snidely failed to give a holiday bonus to, Regis asked him why he kept harassing him and why he didn't receive a bonus. Snidely responded, "I don't like queers, and I don't give them bonuses." That was the last straw, so Regis went to Snidely's boss and complained that Snidely was sexually harassing him. The boss asked Regis whether he had confronted Snidely about it, and Regis said no—he was afraid to say anything to Snidely directly. The boss then told him there was nothing he could do about the situation, and that Regis would just have to be a man and deal with it himself. Regis quit and sued Gizmo Co., Snidely, and Snidely's boss for sexual harassment. Discuss the merits of Regis's claim and what facts and law there are to support it, as well as all possible defenses.

Hypothetical Case

The Vegetarian Bar and Grill has fifty-one employees, most of whom are members of the Church of Ahimsa. The Grill posts a job advertisement seeking a day shift manager and Sam, Sheldon, and Sally all apply. Sam is thirty-two years old and manages an electronics store. He heard about the job from a fellow Church of Ahimsa member who works as a bartender at the Grill. Sheldon and Sally responded to the online advertisement. Sheldon is forty-five years old and has twelve years of experience as a restaurant manager but was recently laid off, while Sally is forty-two and has been the night manager at a local restaurant for sixteen years.

Sally increasingly finds it difficult to care for her young child while working nights and really wants to find a day job. All three candidates are interviewed by the restaurant owner, and Sam is offered and accepts the position. During the interview, the owner asked each candidate the same questions, one of which was, "What would you do if a deer ran out in front of your car and there were trees on both sides of the road?" Both Sheldon and Sally answer that they would hit the deer rather than risk more serious injury by swerving and hitting the trees. Sam answered, "As a member of the Church of Ahimsa, I cannot injure an animal, so I would swerve and hit the tree." When Sheldon and Sally learned that Sam got the job and they didn't, and that most all employees are members of the Church of Ahimsa, they both sued. Sheldon sued for age and religious discrimination and Sally sued for age, gender, and religious discrimination. What are the arguments for and against Sheldon and Sally's positions?

Chapter 31
Negotiable Instruments

Introduction

What is a negotiable instrument? A *negotiable instrument* is a form of commercial paper that provides an unconditional written promise to pay a specific sum of money. Negotiable instruments are a used as a substitute for money. They greatly facilitate business transactions. Checks, promissory notes, and certificates of deposit are all examples of negotiable instruments.

There are two kinds of commercial paper: negotiable and nonnegotiable. Article 3 of the Uniform Commercial Code governs negotiable instruments, which is the subject of this chapter, while ordinary contract law governs nonnegotiable instruments. Although negotiable instruments are not themselves a contract, they are often issued to fulfill a contract. For example, if Sam enters into a contract to buy a car from Sally for $5,000 and he gives her a promissory note for $5,000 when he takes possession of the car, the note is used to fulfill his obligation to pay under the contract, but it is not the contract.

There are two types of negotiable instruments: notes and drafts. The difference between them is that a note is a promise to pay, while a draft is an order requiring someone else to pay.

The transfer of a negotiable instrument, by delivery or endorsement and delivery, gives the new holder the right to enforce payment in his or her own name.

Promissory Notes

A promissory note is a promise to pay money. It is used in virtually every loan transaction regardless of the amount borrowed. A promissory note may be due at a definite date in the future, or the maker may have to pay the note whenever asked (on demand).

If a note is made by a bank, it is called a certificate of deposit (CD). Whenever investors loan money to the bank, the bank gives them a note promising to repay the amount loaned at a specified date in the future. The bank is the maker of the note and the investor is the payee of the note.

Drafts

A draft is an order that directs someone else to pay money to a person. A check is the most commonly used form of a draft. A check is an order telling a bank to pay money to the payee. The drawer (person writing the check) orders the drawee (bank) to pay money to the payee (person to whom the check is written). An example is when you write a check to the student bookstore for the purchase of your textbooks. You are the drawer, the bookstore is the payee, and the bank at which you have the checking account is the drawee.

Note the distinction in the terminology used between notes and drafts. The person who writes a draft (signs the check) is the drawer, while the person who signs a promissory note is the maker. Sometimes the generic term *issuer* is used to describe either a maker or a drawer.

Negotiability

For commercial paper to work as a substitute for money, it must be easily transferable in the marketplace. This means it must be negotiable. For an instrument to be negotiable, it must meet six criteria that are set forth in the Uniform Commercial Code:

1. The promise or order to pay must be in writing.
2. The instrument must be signed by the maker or drawer.
3. The instrument must contain an unconditional promise or order to pay.
4. The instrument must state a specific sum of money to be paid.
5. The instrument must be payable on demand or at a definite time.
6. The instrument must be payable to the bearer or to order.

It is essential that a negotiable instrument contain language that indicates that it is payable to the person who possesses it. Typical language is, "Payable to the order of . . . ." If an instrument does not meet this requirement, it is not a negotiable instrument and will not be treated as such, even if it has all of the other features of negotiability. The only exception is a check that is payable on demand and drawn on a bank.

Nonnegotiable Commercial Paper

The possessor of nonnegotiable commercial paper has the same rights as the person who made the original contract. The transferee's rights are dependent on the rights of the original party to the contract, which means that if the original party somehow loses its right to be paid, so does the transferee. This reduces the value of nonnegotiable commercial paper, because the transferee cannot be absolutely certain they will be paid.

Negotiable Commercial Paper

The possessor of negotiable commercial paper has more rights than the person who entered into the original contract. The possessor's rights with a negotiable commercial paper are unconditional. Generally, they are not dependent on the rights of the original party to the contract. Therefore, as long as the transferee is a holder in due course, they are entitled to be paid the full amount of the note, regardless of the relationship between the parties.

For example, if Sally buys a used boat from Sam's Marina for $20,000 and signs a promissory note with Sam for $20,000 of the purchase price (thereby promising to pay him the money later), her obligation to pay Sam is contingent on the validity of the underlying contract between them. So if the boat is not as warranted, Sally might not be liable for the full amount of the note. However, if Sam wants money immediately, he may sell Sally's promissory note to Mega Finance Company. The price the finance company is willing to pay for the note will depend on whether the note is negotiable or nonnegotiable. If the note is nonnegotiable, the finance company gets the same rights that Sam had. Thus, if a court were to determine that the boat was not as warranted and is therefore only worth $10,000, then that is all the finance company can get from Sally, even though the note is for $20,000.

If the note is a negotiable commercial paper, then the finance company is entitled to receive the full amount of the note regardless of any claims Sally might have against Sam's Marina. If Sam keeps the note, however, even if it is negotiable, Sally will be able to subtract from what she owes him any amount resulting from his breach of contract because, as the original party to the contract, he is not a holder in due course. As such, the finance company that becomes a holder in due course of a negotiable instrument is in a better position to collect on the note than is the original contracting party.

Holder in Due Course

A holder in due course is anyone in possession of a negotiable instrument that is payable to, or indorsed to, them. They gave something of value for it, and they hold it in good faith.

Holder

For example, if you borrow $100 from your friend Ted and sign a promissory note for the loan that states, "I promise to pay to the order of Ted $100," and you sign your name and give the note to Ted, he is a holder in due course because he is in possession of the instrument, and it is payable to him. If Ted hands the note to his roommate Seth, Seth does not become a holder in due course, because the note is not payable to him. However, if before giving it to Seth, Ted writes on the back of the note, "Pay to the order of Seth," Seth does become a holder in due course if he has given something of value for it. However, if Ted writes, "Pay to the order of Seth," on the back of the note but does not give the note to Seth, Seth will not be a holder in due course.

Value

In addition to actually "holding" the negotiable instrument, a party must have given something of value for it to be considered a holder in due course. Someone who receives a negotiable instrument as a gift has not given any value for it and is not a holder in due course.

Value means that the holder has done something in exchange for receiving the negotiable instrument. For example, if Ted's roommate, Seth, had paid the $200 heating bill that the two of them owed for the apartment, then Seth has done something of value in exchange for receiving the $100 note.

Good Faith

Finally, a person who is a holder in due course must have acquired the instrument in good faith. To determine if the holder qualifies, the holder must satisfy both the subjective and objective tests. The subjective test requires that the holder believes that the transaction was honest. The objective test requires that the transaction appear to be commercially reasonable.

Defenses Against a Holder in Due Course

If a note or draft is transferred to a person who acquires it in good faith, without notice of any defenses to payment, and the person becomes a holder in due course, that person can enforce the instrument without being subject to defenses that the maker of the instrument would be able to assert against the original payee, except for certain "real" defenses, which are rarely applicable.

A real defense is one an issuer may use even against a holder in due course. If the holder is not in due course, the issuer may use both real defenses and personal defenses. Thus, both real and personal defenses may be used against an ordinary holder of commercial paper, but only real defenses can be used against a holder in due course.

Real Defenses

Bankruptcy—If a person lists a promissory note among the debts when filing bankruptcy, the debt will be discharged, even as to the holder in due course.

Forgery—If a payee's name is forged on a note and the note is then sold, the payee is not liable to the holder in due course.

Alteration—If the amount to be paid on a negotiable instrument is wrongfully altered, the holder in due course can only collect the original (legitimate) amount. If the note is incomplete, the holder in due course can collect the full face amount stated, even if the instrument was incorrectly filled in. For example, if Ted writes a promissory note to Seth for $200 and Seth adds another 0 to it so it appears to be a note for $2,000 and he sells the note to a holder in due course, the holder will only be able to recover $200. However, if Ted gives Seth a signed promissory note with no amount owed filled in and Seth writes in $2,000, then a holder in due course could recover $2,000 from Ted. In the case where the amount was changed, Ted was not at fault, but in the case where Ted turned over a blank note, he was at fault, so he will have to pay.

Mental incapacity—As in other contract cases, mental incapacity is deemed to invalidate the underlying transaction. Since such a transaction is void, any negotiable instrument created thereby is void and unenforceable.

Illegality—Just as contracts with incapacitated individuals are void, so are contracts resulting from illegal acts. Thus, a negotiable instrument that is the product of an illegal transaction will be unenforceable even by a holder in due course.

Minority—Since a person under legal age has the right to void a contract, the person is also given the right to avoid paying on a negotiable instrument, even to a holder in due course.

Fraud in the execution—When the issuer has been duped into signing a negotiable instrument without knowing what it is, and with no way of finding out, the court will likely find that it was the result of fraud in the execution of the instrument, and even a holder in due course will not be allowed to recover.

Personal Defenses

These defenses are valid against an ordinary holder, but not a holder in due course.

Breach of contract—If the underlying contract that is the basis for the note is breached (i.e., the odometer of the car purchased has been illegally set back), then the payee can legitimately refuse to pay anyone other than a holder in due course.

Failure of consideration—If a negotiable instrument lacks consideration, a mere holder is not entitled to payment, but a holder in due course is. For example, Sam writes a $500 check to Sally as a gift, but then they have a fight, so he calls the bank and instructs it to stop payment on the check. Since Sally received the check as a gift and gave nothing of value for it, she is a mere holder and has no right to payment. However, if Sally cashes the check before Sam stops payment, he will still have to pay the bank, since the bank has given something of value for it (it paid Sally $500), so it is a holder in due course and is entitled to the money.

Prior payment—If a party pays off a note but does not retrieve it or mark it paid in full, it risks being obligated to pay the amount stated if it is sold to a holder in due course. For example, if Sam buys a car from Seth and gives him a promissory note for it but fails to get the note back or write paid in full on it after he pays it off, he may have to pay the amount again if Seth sells the note for value to Sally, who becomes a holder in due course.

Unauthorized completion—If Sam writes a check to Seth to reimburse him for paying Sam's portion of the electric bill but he fails to fill in the $200 amount owed and Seth writes in $1,000 and cashes the check, Sam will have to pay the bank $1,000, since it paid Seth and is a holder in due course.

Non-delivery—If Sally writes a note that reads "payable to bearer" but she loses it before she gives it to Seth, and Sam finds it and sells it to a finance company for value, Sally will have to pay the finance company, even though she never gave it to the company or intended for it to own the note. However, Sally would not have to pay Sam if he kept the note, since he would be a mere holder and she did not deliver the note to him.

Fraud in the inducement—If a promissory note is given on the basis of fraud, then the payee does not have to pay the holder. But if the holder sells the note for value to a holder in due course, then the payee is obligated to make payment even if the underlying contract was fraudulent. For example, if Sally writes a note for $1,000 and gives it to Sam in exchange for a motorcycle he has already sold to someone else, Sally will not have to pay Sam. However, if Sam sells the note to a finance company for value, Sally will have to pay the finance company because it is a holder in due course.

Outstanding Claims or Other Defects of Negotiable Instruments

Sometimes a holder is aware that an instrument has an outstanding claim against it or some other defect. The most common problems are discussed here.

The Instrument Is Overdue

A check is overdue ninety days after its date. Other demand instruments are overdue one day after a request for payment has been made, or a reasonable time after it has been issued. If an instrument is not paid by the date it is due, the recipient is on notice that it may have a defect. A reasonable person would wonder why no one has attempted to collect the money owed.

The Instrument Is Dishonored

A dishonored instrument is one where the party has refused to pay it. If someone knows that payment has been refused, then the person cannot be a holder in due course. For example, if a bank stamps "insufficient funds" on the back of a check presented for payment, the check has been dishonored and no one who obtains it afterward can be a holder in due course.

The Instrument Is Forged, Altered, or Incomplete

If a holder knows that an instrument has been altered or forged, it cannot be a holder in due course. For example, if Seth writes a check to Sally for $100 but leaves the line for writing out the amount to be paid blank and Sally adds another zero after the number 100 and fills in "one thousand" on the line for writing out the amount while Ted looks on, if she endorses the check over to Ted, he is not a holder in due course because he knows she altered the check. However, if Ted takes the altered check indorsed to him and sells it to the finance company, the finance company becomes a holder in due course because it did not know the check was altered.

The Holder Is Aware of Claims or Defenses

A holder in due course cannot be someone who has notice that someone else has a claim to the instrument or that there is a dispute between the original parties to the instrument. For example, Seth agrees to buy a used car from Sally and signs a $5,000 note to her for it when she no longer owns the car. If Sally tries to sell the note to her uncle who knows she obtained the note fraudulently, he will not be considered a holder in due course if he buys the note, since he is aware of the fraud.

The Shelter Rule

Typically, if a holder is not a holder in due course, he cannot recover any money if the person primarily or secondarily responsible can set up a defense to the claim that money is owed. A holder who is not a holder in due course is subject to the same defenses as if the person possessed a nonnegotiable instrument. The only exception to this is a holder who is not a holder in due course but who derived title from a holder in due course. In this instance, the shelter rule is applicable.

Under the shelter rule, the person who transfers an instrument passes on all of the rights. When a holder in due course transfers an instrument, the recipient acquires all the same rights—even if the recipient is not a holder in due course.

For example, Consumer Products rebate center sent Sally a check for $200 as a rebate for her purchase of a large-screen TV. Sally claimed that she never got the check so Consumer Products stopped payment on the check and sent her another one. However, Sally took the first check and signed it over to Fred, her car mechanic, for work he did fixing her car. At this point, Fred is a holder in due course and is entitled to payment from Consumer Products. However, instead of Fred attempting to cash the check himself, he sells it to a finance company, which knows that the check has been dishonored but buys it anyway. Under the Shelter Rule, the finance company acquired Fred's rights as a holder in due course and is entitled to payment.

The point of the shelter rule is not to benefit the likes of the finance company, but instead, to protect those in the position of Fred. The law is based on the premise that it would not do Fred any good to be a holder in due course if he could not sell the instrument to anyone. There is one exception to this rule, however; if a holder in due course transfers the instrument to a prior holder who was a party to the fraud involving that instrument (i.e., Sally), that prior holder does not acquire the rights of a holder in due course.

Hypothetical Case

Sally wants to buy the house Fred is selling, but her credit isn't good enough to get a mortgage, so Fred agrees to sell it to her on a land contract. She signs a promissory note to him for the $75,000 purchase price. Fred promptly sells the note and indorses it to the Acme Finance Co. for $70,000. Six months later, Sally finds out that there is a lien on the property for $4,000 in back taxes that Fred failed to pay. Since Fred never disclosed this material fact to her, Sally wants to rescind the contract. If she is successful, will she be liable to Acme Finance Co. for $75,000? Why or why not?

Chapter 32
Liability for Negotiable Instruments

Introduction

A person or company who purchases a negotiable instrument in the ordinary course of business can reasonably expect that it will be paid when presented to the maker without worrying about becoming involved in a dispute between the maker and the person to whom the instrument was first issued.

Sometimes, however, the issuer of an instrument believes it has been defrauded or otherwise unfairly dealt with by the payee and may refuse to pay the holder in due course, which results in a lawsuit to recover on the instrument.

Although a negotiable instrument is a promise to pay a sum of money, it is not a contract. A contract requires offer, acceptance, and consideration, which a negotiable instrument does not have. Also, unlike a contract, the right to payment of a negotiable instrument is tied to possession of the document itself. The rights of the holder in due course (payee) are actually better than those provided by a contract. This is because the right to payment is not dependent on the validity of the underlying contract that gave rise to the debt. It is also possible for the holder in due course to have better title than the party the holder obtains the instrument from if the transferee becomes a party to the contract and is able to enforce the contract in the holder's own name.

Not everyone who signs a negotiable instrument is an issuer, and not everyone who presents an instrument for payment is a holder. There is, however, liability for people who sign a negotiable instrument, just as there is liability for non-holders who receive payment. The liability pertaining to someone who has signed an instrument is referred to as *signature liability*, and the liability of someone who receives payment is called *warranty liability*. These and other forms of liability for negotiable instruments are discussed next.

Signature Liability

Everyone who signs a negotiable instrument is potentially liable for it, but the degree of liability depends on the person's capacity when it was signed. For example, the liability of the maker of a note is different than the liability of someone who indorses the note.

The Maker's Liability

The maker (issuer) is primarily liable for the note since the maker is the one who has promised to pay and must pay unless the maker has a valid defense. Thus, no one is primarily liable for a check written on a bank account until the bank accepts it.

The Drawer's Liability

The drawer is the person who writes the check and he or she has secondary liability. The drawer is not liable until he or she receives notice that the bank has dishonored the check. If the bank pays the check with the drawer's funds, the drawer will become secondarily liable only if the bank dishonors the check. For example, if Sam writes Sally a $5,000 check to pay for the car he just bought from her and Sally asks him if his check is good and he replies, "You don't think I'd write a bad check do you?" Sally has no recourse against him. But if she attempts to cash the check and the bank teller informs her that there are insufficient funds in Sam's account to cover the check, then Sam is liable to Sally for the $5,000.

The Drawee's Liability

The drawee is the bank on which the check is drawn. It is incorrect to assume that just because the drawer of the check is secondarily liable, the drawee bank is primarily liable. Unfortunately, when the drawer signs the check, it enters a no-man's land. The bank is not liable to the holder and has no liability for damages to the holder for refusing to pay the check. It is possible that the bank will be liable to the drawer for violating their checking account agreement, but this agreement does not apply to the holder of the check. As such, the bank can either pay the check or dishonor it. If the bank dishonors it, the holder must pursue remedies against the drawer. This is because under the UCC, a bank is not liable on a check until it accepts the check for payment. If it refuses to accept it when the account has sufficient funds, the holder has no claim against the bank because there is no privity between the parties. The holder only has a claim against the issuer of the check. The issuer may then have a claim against his bank.

The Indorser's Liability

The indorser is anyone other than the issuer who signs the negotiable instrument. Indorsers are secondarily liable. As such, the indorser must pay if the issuer or drawee does not. There are four exceptions to this however:

1. The bank issues a certified check.
2. The check is presented for payment more than thirty days after it is indorsed.
3. The check is dishonored and the indorser is not notified within thirty days.
4. The indorser writes "without recourse" next to his or her signature.

The Accommodation Party's Liability

The accommodation party is the party who adds its signature to a negotiable instrument for the purpose of being liable on it. Usually, the accommodation party does not receive any direct benefit from the negotiable instrument but agrees to be liable for it solely to accommodate the other party. For example, when Sam attempts to buy a truck from Fred's Used Cars, Fred will not sell accept a promissory note from him unless he has someone else also sign it who agrees to pay if Sam does not. Sam gets his father to agree to sign as a "co-signer" on the note. Sam is the accommodated party and Sam's father is the accommodation party.

An accommodation party has the same liability to the holder as the person for whom he signed. Therefore, if Sam fails to pay on the promissory note, the holder can make a claim directly against Sam's father without first demanding payment from Sam. If Sam's father is forced to pay the note, however, he may try to recover the money from Sam.

Warranty Liability

As mentioned previously, if someone forges a person's name to a negotiable instrument, the forger will be responsible for it and not the person whose name was forged. The drawee bank is liable if it pays a check on which the drawee's name is forged, and in other cases of wrongdoing, the person who first acquires an instrument from a wrongdoer is ultimately liable to anyone who pays value for it.

Transfer Warranties

A person who transfers an instrument promises that it is valid and warrants the following:

- They are a holder of the instrument.
- The instrument has not been altered.
- All signatures are authentic and authorized.
- As far as the person knows, the issuer is solvent.
- No defense can be asserted against them.

Presentment Warranties

Presentment warranties protect those who demand payment for an instrument from the maker, drawee, or anyone else liable on it.

When individuals present a check for payment, they warrant that they are a holder, the check has not been altered, and that they have no reason to believe the drawer's signature has been forged.

The presentment warranty for a promissory note is different than it is for a check. A person who presents a promissory note for payment only makes one warranty—that he is the holder of the instrument. If someone presents a note with a forged signature, the person is violating the presentment warranty because a forged signature prevents subsequent owners from being holders.

Other Liability Rules

There are several other rules that impose liability on parties who wrongfully create, pay or redeem negotiable instruments. These rules are discussed below.

Negligence

This rule holds a person liable for negligently creating or paying an unauthorized negotiable instrument to an innocent third party.

Imposter Rule

Even though someone issues a negotiable instrument to an imposter, any indorsement in the name of the payee is valid as long as the person (bank) who pays the instrument does not know of the fraud. For example, someone knocks on your door claiming to be selling extended car warranties from Longterm Warranty Co., and you sign up and give the salesman a $200 check made payable to Longterm Warranty Co. If there is no Longterm Warranty Co. and the salesperson forges an indorsement in the name of the company and cashes the check, the bank will not be liable for cashing it. The law considers that those who actually dealt with the imposter are in a better position to determine if they were perpetrating a fraud than is the bank.

Fictitious Payee Rule

If an instrument is issued to a non-existent person, then the indorsement in the name of the payee is valid as long as the person (bank) who pays it does not know of the fraud. For example, if in the course of paying the company's bills Sally writes out monthly checks to "Sue Smith" and then cashes them herself, the company can hold her liable but not the bank for cashing them.

Employee Indorsement Rule

If an employee who is responsible for issuing instruments forges a check or other negotiable instrument, any indorsement in the name of the payee, or similar name, is valid as long as the person (bank) who pays the instrument does not know of the fraud. For example, Sally is employed as the treasurer for NewAge Corporation, and once a month, in addition to paying the company's bills, she writes herself a check for $1,000 and forges the name of the company vice president on it, since his signature is required for any check larger than $500. If she successfully cashes these checks, the bank will not be liable since she had the general authority to sign company checks and it was not aware of her forgery. If Sally worked as a company janitor, the bank would be liable for the checks—but because she had authority to sign them, it bears no liability failing to determine the validity of the additional signature.

Discharge

An instrument is discharged when liability for it terminates. Almost any change in an instrument that harms an indorser or accommodation party has the consequence of discharging their obligation. This is true unless the party consented to the change.

The UCC identifies five ways in which an instrument is discharged:

1. By making proper payment.
2. By agreement. The parties to the instrument can agree to discharge it even if the instrument is not paid.
3. By cancellation. This is accomplished by the intentional and voluntary surrender, destruction, or disfigurement of the instrument.
4. By certification. When a bank certifies or accepts a check, the drawer and all indorsers of it are discharged and only the bank is liable.
5. By alteration. If the terms of the instrument are intentionally changed, it is discharged.

Liability by Banks and Bank Customers

Perhaps the most common negotiable instrument is a bank check. Because they are so relied on for both business and personal transactions there are many rules dealing with their use. The most common are discussed below.

Checking Accounts

Whenever you deposit money in a checking account, the bank owes you money. It becomes a debtor to you. The bank also serves as your agent since you have authorized it to represent you in certain legal capacities.

A bank has a duty to pay a check if it is authorized by the customer and conforms to the terms of the bank's checking account agreement. If a bank violates this duty and wrongfully dishonors an authorized check, it is liable to the customer for all actual and consequential damages.

Electronic Banking and Electronic Fund Transfers

The Electronic Fund Transfer Act (EFTA) was passed to protect consumers in their dealings with banks. It defines a consumer as anyone who is a natural person, thus excluding corporations and businesses. It establishes time frames under which a person's account must be credited with a deposit and when those funds may be withdrawn.

Employers are not allowed to require that employees receive their paychecks by electronic transfer to a particular bank—but they are allowed to require that employees receive them electronically at some bank.

Death of a Customer

When a bank customer dies, the bank may continue to pay checks on their account for ten days after it learns of their death, unless it receives a stop payment order from someone claiming an interest in the account. Typically, however, banks freeze checking accounts as soon as they learn of the account holder's death.

Incompetent Customers

As soon as a bank is notified that a court has ruled that a customer is incompetent, it is to freeze the account and will be held liable if it pays the customer's checks.

Forgery

If a bank pays a forged check, either the bank or the customer will lose money; the UCC decided that the bank should bear this risk more so than the customer. Therefore, if a bank pays a check on which the issuer's name is forged, it must re-credit the issuer's account.

Alteration

With only one exception, if a bank pays a check that has been altered, the customer is only liable for the original amount of the check and the bank is liable for the balance. The exception is if the alteration is obvious; then the bank will be held liable for the full amount of the check because it should have known better than to cash it.

Completion

If a check is incomplete and someone other than the original issuer fills it in, the bank is not liable unless it was on notice that the completion was unauthorized.

Stale Checks

A bank does not have to pay checks that are presented more than six months after their date. If it does pay a check after more than six months, it is not liable.

Post-Dated Checks

A check that is presented for payment before its date is a post-dated check. For example, if Sally writes a check to Sam for the bicycle she is buying from and dates it the following Friday because that is her payday and he tries to cash it immediately, he is attempting to cash a post-dated check.

A bank is not liable for paying a post-dated check unless the customer has notified the bank in advance that a post-dated check is coming. So if Sally tells Sam, "Don't cash this check until next Friday, when my paycheck will be deposited," and he tells her, "Hey, I already gave you the bike, so I can cash the check," she should call her bank and warn that a post-dated check made payable to Sam is going to be presented for payment.

Stop Payment Orders

Checks that were authorized when issued may still be nullified by the customer. Generally, if a bank pays a check when a customer has given it a stop payment order, it will be liable for any loss the customer suffers.

An oral stop payment order is only valid for fourteen days while a written order expires after six months. Thus, if a customer does not renew the stop payment order (usually at a cost), a person may be successful in cashing the check when the stop payment order expires.

A stop payment order is only valid if it describes the check with reasonable certainly and the bank receives the stop payment order before it pays the check.

Customer's Right to Withdraw Funds

The Expedited Funds Availability Act (EFAA) specifies the maximum time a bank can hold funds deposited by check before allowing a customer to withdraw them. Under this statute, a customer must wait longer to withdraw cash from funds deposited by check than they have to wait to write checks on them. This is because banks are at greater risk when customers withdraw cash than they are when they write a check.

Customer's Liability for Unauthorized Transactions

If a thief steals your ATM card or debit card, it is important to report it to the bank immediately. This is because if the theft is reported to the bank within two days, you will only be responsible for the first $50 fraudulently charged on the account. If the theft is reported after two days but within sixty days of receiving a bank statement that shows the unauthorized withdrawal, you will be responsible for a maximum of $500. After sixty days, you will be liable for the full amount of any fraudulent charges.

Sometimes a fraudulent transfer of funds takes place without the use of a stolen card. In that situation, consumers are not liable at all as long as they report the loss within sixty days of receiving a bank statement that shows the loss. If, however, more than sixty days pass and the consumer has not reported the fraudulent transaction they will be liable for the entire amount.

Customer's Duty to Examine Bank Statements

Customers have a duty to read over their bank statements and look for forged or altered checks. A failure to report a forgery or alteration more than a year after its appearance on the statement eliminates any liability the bank may have. If a customer fails to notify the bank of a forgery or alteration within thirty days of receiving a statement, the bank will be relieved from liability for cashing any subsequent checks by the same forger.

Hypothetical Case

Sam treats Sally to dinner for her birthday and uses his MasterCard to pay for it. After filling in the tip amount and signing the charge slip, he forgets to put it in his wallet and leaves it in the restaurant. The busboy picks it up as he's busing the table and puts it in his pocket. A few days later, the busboy uses the information on the charge slip to order over $1,000 worth of merchandise from various Internet sites that he has sent to a fictitious name but real address. Sam doesn't realize anything is amiss until he gets his MasterCard statement three weeks later. He immediately calls the number on his MasterCard and reports the transactions he did not make. What, if any, of the fraudulent charges will Sam be responsible for paying? What, if any, of the fraudulent charges will the bank be responsible for paying?

Chapter 33
Secured Transactions

Introduction

What are secured transactions? A *secured transaction* is one in which a creditor takes an interest in a piece of property that is used as collateral for a loan. This interest is referred to as a security interest. The most common example of a secured transaction is the typical automobile purchase. The average purchaser of a new car does not have enough money to pay cash for the vehicle and must take out a loan to pay for it. The financial institution that loans the buyer money takes a security interest in the car that is being purchased with the money it is loaning. This is done through a contract called a *security agreement,* and the car is the collateral for the loan. The result is if the buyer fails to make the car payments as required, the financial institution will exercise its rights under the security agreement and will obtain possession of the car, sell it for what it can, and hold the purchaser liable for any remaining deficiency.

Article 9 of the UCC

Article 9 of the UCC governs secured transactions in personal property and applies to any transaction intended to create a security interest in personal property or fixtures. Specifically, it recognizes several types of personal property that may be used as collateral:

- Goods—property that is movable
- Inventory—goods held by someone for sale or lease, such as automobiles for sale at a dealership
- Instruments—drafts, checks, promissory notes, and certificates of deposit
- Investment property—usually refers to securities
- Other property—includes accounts, intellectual property, documents of title, and chattel paper

Article 9 uses other terms that most people are unfamiliar with, which are defined here.

Authentication—Authentication occurs when a person signs a document by using a method that identifies them and indicates they are adopting the record as their own.

Collateral—Collateral is the property that is the subject of the security interest. For example, the automobile company that finances your car purchase will keep a security interest in the vehicle, which is the collateral.

Debtor—The debtor is the person who has an original ownership interest in the collateral. One example is the person who buys the car with the loan from the automobile dealership.

Financing statement—The financing statement is a written document that notifies the general public that the secured party has a security interest in the collateral.

Fixtures—Fixtures are goods that are attached to real estate. For example, a ceiling fan is a good when the company makes and sells it, but once it is installed in a house it becomes a fixture.

Perfection—Perfection is a series of steps the secured party takes to protect its rights in the collateral against all others outside of the debtor.

Record—The record is the information about the transaction that is written on paper or stored in electronic form.

Security agreement—The security agreement is the contract by which the debtor gives a security interest to the secured party. It protects the secured party's rights in the collateral.

Security interest—A security interest is the interest in personal property or fixtures that "secures" the performance of the debtor's obligation. The automobile dealership's security interest in the car it sold you is what gives it the legal right to repossess the car and sell it if you don't make the required payments.

Secured party—The secured party is the person or company that holds the security interest. The automobile dealership that sells you a car and finances it for you is the secured party.

Attaching a Security Interest

Attachment is an essential part of every secured transaction. Under Article 9 of the UCC, attachment means that the secured party has performed three necessary steps to create an enforceable security interest:

1. The parties have made a security agreement, and either the debtor has authenticated a security agreement describing the collateral or the secured party has obtained possession of the collateral.
2. The secured party has given something of value to obtain the security agreement.
3. The debtor has rights in the collateral.

Obviously, if there is no agreement there can be no security interest. In most instances, the agreement must be in writing and signed by the debtor. It may be electronically recorded and authenticated by the debtor. The collateral must be identified in the agreement.

There are a few situations where the security agreement does not have to be in writing. One occurs when the parties have an oral security agreement and the secured party has possession of the collateral. This often occurs during stock purchases where the purchaser typically leaves the stock certificates in the possession of the secured party.

Perfection

When the security interest has attached to the collateral, the secured party is protected against the debtor. For example, when the security interest in the automobile being purchased is perfected, the dealership may take possession of it if the purchaser fails to make the required payments. There are three ways a security interest may be perfected:

1. Perfection by filing
2. Perfection by possession
3. Perfection of consumer goods

In some instances, a secured party may choose which method to use, but in others only one method will work.

Perfection by Filing

The most commonly used method is perfection by filing. This is done by filing a financing statement with the appropriate state agency. The financing statement lists the names of all parties to the agreement, describes the collateral, and gives enough information about the security interest to enable any interested person to learn about it. If the financing statement does not contain enough information to put people on notice of the security interest or it fails to file it with the right agency, its interests may be challenged and fail.

A financing statement is usually deemed sufficient if it includes the name of the debtor, the name of the secured party, and an indication of the collateral. The location where financing statements must be filed vary from state to state so it is essential to check the law of the applicable state.

Perfection by Possession

For most types of collateral it is permissible to perfect by possession in addition to filing. For example, if the collateral is a diamond ring, the jewelry store that loaned the money to buy it may perfect its security interest by holding the ring until the loan is paid off. When the secured party retains the collateral, however, it has a duty to use reasonable care in preserving and protecting the collateral in its possession.

Perfection of Consumer Goods

The UCC contains special provisions for security interests in the most common consumer goods, which are those used primarily for personal, family, or household purposes. This is because it is impractical and unworkable for merchants to file a financing statement for every piece of furniture or electronic equipment for which a consumer owes money. To deal with this, the UCC recognizes a purchase money security interest (PMSI), which is taken by the party who sells the collateral or the party who advances money so the debtor can buy the collateral. A PMSI in consumer goods perfects automatically and requires no filing.

A PMSI is only applicable when the money loaned is used to purchase a consumer good that is used as collateral. It cannot, for instance, be used in situations where the money loaned is used to purchase a business's inventory.

Buyer Protections

A buyer in the ordinary course of business (BIOC) is someone who buys goods in good faith from a seller who routinely deals in such goods. For example, Sam's Fish Market buys fifty whitefish from Marquette Fisheries. Sam's Market is a BIOC. He is buying in good faith and Marquette Fisheries routinely deals in whitefish. This status is important because a BIOC is generally not affected by security interests in goods. However, if a buyer is aware that the seller has violated another party's rights in the goods, then the buyer would not be acting in good faith and the rule would not apply. Typically, however, a BIOC takes the goods free of a security interest created by the seller, even though the security interest may be perfected.

Once a security interest is perfected, it remains in effect regardless of whether the collateral is sold or transferred. For example, Sally borrows $100,000 from Mega Finance Co. to keep her lawn service company in business, and the finance company takes a security interest in the twenty industrial lawn mowers that her company owns. A few months later, she needs still more cash so she sells five of the lawn mowers to Jack's Lawn Service Co. Unfortunately, even that isn't enough, and six months later, she files for bankruptcy. Will Mega Finance Co. be able to obtain the five lawn mowers Sally sold to Jack's? Yes, it will. The security interest Mega Finance Co. had in the lawn mowers continued even after Jack's purchased them, and the finance company may take possession once Sally defaults on her loan payments.

Priorities Among Creditors

Sometimes, two creditors have a security interest in the same collateral. What happens then? Quite often, the debtor doesn't have enough assets to pay everyone, so all the creditors compete to be first to be paid. The UCC has rules dictating how this situation should be handled.

The first rule is that a party with a perfected security interest takes priority over a party with an unperfected security interest. The whole point of perfecting a security interest is to ensure that your security interest gets priority over everyone else's.

The second rule is that if neither secured party has a perfected security interest, the first interest to attach will be given priority.

The third, and final, rule is that between perfected security interests, the first party that filed or perfected its interest gets paid first.

Debtor Default

If the debtor fails to perform its obligations or has defaulted, the security agreement may terminate. Usually, the parties will define what constitutes a default in their security agreement. Most always, one instance of default is a failure of the debtor to make the payments required. Whatever is defined as a default, when it occurs, the secured party has two options: (1) it may take possession of the collateral, or (2) it may file suit against the debtor for the money owed.

If the debtor defaults, the secured party may take possession of the collateral without any court order, provided it can do so without any breach of the peace. Once the secured party obtains the collateral, it may dispose of it or retain it as full satisfaction of the debt. Until the secured party disposes of the collateral the debtor has the right to redeem it by paying the full amount owed on the debt. If they pay the debt they may retrieve the collateral.

If the secured party sells the collateral, it applies the proceeds first to its expenses in repossessing and selling the collateral and second to the debt. Often, there is a deficiency, meaning the proceeds from the sale are not sufficient to pay off all of the debt. If this happens, the debtor remains liable for the deficiency and the creditor will sue to collect it.

If the debtor pays off the debt, the secured party must complete a termination statement, which is a document stating that it no longer claims a security interest in the collateral.

Hypothetical Case

Adam owns a small hotel and decides he needs to update all of its furnishings. He goes to Ted's Furniture Store and buys $100,000 worth of new furniture. Ted's Furniture finances the purchase and retains a security interest in the furniture. Adam begins making the required $2,000 a month payments on the loan and remains current until a fire destroys half of his hotel rooms (and their new furniture). After Adam misses three payments in a row, Ted's Furniture declares him in default. What actions is Ted's Furniture likely to take, and why? Is there additional information that, if demonstrated, might produce different results? If so, explain.

Chapter 34
Business Organization

Introduction

There are many different ways to set up a new business. Each new business owner must decide which is best for that business. The first thing a new business owner must decide is whether the business will be for profit or not for profit. This is important because it affects the way you will organize your business. Being a not-for-profit business does not mean the business cannot pay its employees good salaries or be highly successful. It does mean that the business must meet certain criteria established by the Internal Revenue Service to avoid paying taxes on income. Depending on the purpose for which the business is formed, it may or may not be entitled to non-profit status. Most businesses are organized and run as for-profit businesses, so we will discuss those.

Sole Proprietorship

Sole proprietorships are the most common form of business organizations. They are the easiest and most common form of for-profit businesses. A sole proprietorship is an unincorporated business owned by one person. The owner may operate the business alone or may employ others. The owner of the sole proprietorship business has total and unlimited personal liability for all debts incurred by the business.

Sole proprietorships are the easiest and least expensive business form to create and operate. The disadvantage of a sole proprietorship is that the owner is personally liable for all debt and all tort and contract lawsuits or judgments of the business.

Partnerships

A partnership is a form of business which two or more people operate for the common goal of making a profit. Each partner has total and unlimited personal liability for the debts incurred by the partnership.

There are three classifications of partnerships: general partnerships, limited partnerships, and limited liability partnerships.

General Partnership

A general partnership, or simply a partnership, refers to an association of persons or an unincorporated company with three features:

1. It may be created by agreement, proof of existence, or estoppel.
2. It is formed by two or more persons.
3. The owners are all personally liable for any legal actions and debts the company incurs.

In most states, a written document is not necessary to form a general partnership, but a written agreement is still a good idea, especially in addressing management issues.

The advantages of a general partnership are that they are easy to form, and they do not pay taxes. The disadvantage of a partnership is that each partner is personally liable for the debts of the partnership, regardless of how or who incurred them. Also, financing a partnership may be difficult because the firm cannot sell shares in itself the way a corporation can. Therefore, the capital needs of the partnership must be met by the partners or by borrowing the money. In addition, all partners have an equal say in running the business, unless there is an agreement to the contrary, which can often lead to management paralysis.

Transferability

A partner may only transfer the value of his or her partnership interest. Partners cannot transfer their interest in the partnership itself. For example, a parent may give a child the value of the partnership interest, but not the right to be a partner in the business.

Partnership Taxes

A partnership is not a taxable entity, so it does not pay taxes itself. All income and losses of the partnership are passed on to the partners, and they must report them on their personal income tax returns.

Termination of the Partnership

Typically, a partnership terminates upon the death, disability, or withdrawal of any of the partners. However, most partnership agreements provide for these events by stating that the share of the departed partner can be purchased by the remaining partners.

Profits

Partnership profits are shared equally amongst the partners unless there is an agreement that expressly provides for a different manner of sharing the business's profits and losses.

Adding Partners

Unless otherwise provided in the partnership agreement, no one can become a member of the partnership without the consent of all partners.

Limited Partnership

A limited partnership is similar to a general partnership, except that in addition to one or more general partners, there are also one or more limited partners.

The general partners have management control, share the right to use partnership property, share the profits of the firm in predefined proportions, and have joint and several liability for the debts of the partnership. The limited partners, however, are only liable on debts incurred by the firm to the extent of their registered investment, and they have no management authority. The general partners pay the limited partners a return on their investment as defined in the partnership agreement.

Limited partners must usually file documents with the state in which they disclose their limited partner status so that third parties have notice that parties dealing with the partnership or these individuals are aware of their limited liability. Unlike the general partners, limited partners do not have inherent agency authority to bind the firm unless they are held out as agents and thereby create an agency by estoppel.

Some common limited partnership uses are found in the film industry, where it works well for the purpose of making a move. Real estate investment projects or other businesses that focus on a single or limited-term project are other examples where limited partnerships work well. The limited partnership is also attractive to firms wishing to provide shares to many individuals without the additional tax liability of a corporation.

Limited Liability Partnerships

A limited liability partnership (LLP) has elements of both partnerships and corporations. In an LLP, partners are not liable for another partner's misconduct or negligence. This is an important difference from that of a limited partnership. In an LLP, all partners have a form of limited liability for each individual's protection within the partnership. This distinction of granting limited liability to all partners, not just a subset of non-managing "limited partners," makes the LLP more suited for businesses where all investors wish to take an active role in management.

The LLP is an especially popular form of organization among professionals, particularly lawyers, accountants, and architects. This is because each partner may take an active management role in the business while not becoming personally liable, directly or indirectly, for an obligation solely because the person is a partner.

Profits

As in a partnership or Limited Liability Company, the profits of an LLP are allocated among the partners for tax purposes, thus avoiding the problem of double taxation often found in corporations.

Disadvantages

There are five disadvantages of an LLP:

1. There are restrictions on ownership.
2. LLPs retain liability for improper distributions.
3. Partnership interests are not as freely transferable.
4. There is a minimum number of owners.
5. Merger opportunities are limited.

Terminating an LLP

An LLP may be terminated by the death or dissociation of a partner. However, a partner who dissociates (quits) may have to pay damages to the remaining partners if this departure caused harm to the partnership.

A partnership may also be ended by dissolution. The rules governing dissolution depend on the type of partnership. If the partners have agreed in advance on how long the partnership will last, it is a *term partnership*. Otherwise it is a partnership *at will*, which means any partner may leave at any time. The partnership automatically ends when a partner leaves.

A term partnership automatically ends when any of four conditions are met:

1. All partners agree to dissolve.
2. The term expires or the partnership goals are achieved.
3. A partner leaves and the remaining partners vote to dissolve.
4. The partnership business becomes illegal, such as when exporting goods to an embargoed country.

Corporations

A business corporation is a for-profit, limited liability entity that has a separate legal existence from its members. A corporation is owned by multiple shareholders and is overseen by a board of directors, which hires the people who manage the business. The defining feature of a corporation is that it has a legal existence that is independent from the people who create it. If a corporation fails, shareholders will only lose their investment, and employees will lose their jobs, but neither will be liable for the debts that are owed to the corporation's creditors. Thus, a corporation has limited liability.

The creation and existence of corporations is governed by statute, which balances the interests of the shareholders who invest their money in them and the employees who run them.

Because corporations are granted an independent legal existence, they are recognized by law to have rights and responsibilities like actual people. Corporations can exercise human rights against real individuals and the state and they may be held responsible for human rights violations. Corporations can even be convicted of criminal offenses, such as fraud and manslaughter.

Also, because the corporation is treated as a fictional person, it can own property, enter into contracts, and pay taxes in a capacity that is separate from that of its shareholders. This independent legal personality has two economic implications. First, it grants creditors priority over the corporate assets upon its liquidation, and second, corporate assets cannot be withdrawn by its shareholders, nor can the assets of the corporation be taken by personal creditors of its shareholders.

Benefits of a Corporation

Unlike a partnership or sole proprietorship, shareholders of a corporation have "limited" liability for the corporation's debts and obligations. As a result, shareholders' losses cannot exceed the amount that they paid for stock shares. The economic rationale for this is that it allows anonymous trading in the shares of the corporation by eliminating the corporation's creditors as a stakeholder in the transaction. Without limited liability, a creditor would probably not allow any share to be sold to a buyer who did not have at least the same creditworthiness as the seller.

Limited liability also allows corporations to raise significantly more money for its projects by combining funds from the owners of stock. Since limited liability reduces the amount that a shareholder can lose in a company, it greatly reduces the risk for potential shareholders and increases both their number and the amount they are likely to invest.

Another advantage of the corporation is that its assets and structure exist beyond the lifetime of any of its shareholders, bondholders, or employees. This provides stability and allows the accumulation of capital, which can then be used to invest in projects of a larger size and over a longer term than if the business were subject to dissolution and distribution.

Disadvantages of a Corporation

There are certain disadvantages to a corporation, of course. Because their existence is entirely controlled by statute, there are many more formalities to their creation, which necessarily results in greater costs and fees. Under some state statutes the names of corporate officers must be disclosed, which may discourage some people from serving. Also, because a corporation has a distinct legal existence, it must pay taxes on its income, and the tax rate for corporations can be much higher than for individuals or other business forms. In addition, there is the problem of double taxation, which occurs when the corporation pays taxes on its income and then the shareholders pay taxes when some of that income is distributed to them in the form of dividends.

Corporation Status

Although corporations are created by filing the requisite documents with a particular state government, the Internal Revenue Service grants them specific tax designations under the Internal Revenue Code.

C Corporations

A C corporation is not actually a business structure, but the tax status of the company as defined by the Internal Revenue Code (IRC). This is also true of S corporations.

A C corporation is a general for-profit corporation. It is the "default" status for all corporations under the IRC. Like all corporations, C corporations are required to pay taxes on the income they generate.

When a corporation is formed, it is formed as a C corporation and then has the option of claiming S corporation status. All corporations are C corporations unless they decide to take advantage of a provision in both federal and state tax laws to become an S corporation.

S Corporations

S corporations were created by Congress to encourage entrepreneurship through special tax breaks. The shareholders in S corporations enjoy the limited liability of a corporation *and* the tax status of a partnership. An S corporation is not a taxable entity, and all of its profits and losses are passed through to its shareholders, who pay taxes at their individual rates. Thus, if a start-up S corporation loses money, its investors can deduct the corporation's loses against their other income.

The Limitations of an S Corporation

Although an S corporation has many attractive characteristics, its limitations often result in a different corporate election. Five of the more significant S corporation limitations are as follows:

1. There can only be one class of stock.
2. There can be only one hundred shareholders.
3. Shareholders must be U.S. citizens or residents.
4. Shareholders must be individuals, estates, charities, pension funds, or trusts. They cannot be partnerships or other corporations.
5. All shareholders must agree that the company should be an S corporation.

The main difference between a C corporation and an S corporation is the way the corporation is taxed. A C corporation is taxed as an incorporated business and an S corporation is taxed as a partnership or a sole proprietorship.

Close Corporations

The majority of corporations are said to be closely held, privately held, or close corporations. This means that their stock shares are not publicly traded. The requirements for a close corporation differ in each state, but generally it must meet four criteria:

1. It must protect minority shareholders.
2. There must be some transfer restrictions for the sale of stock shares.
3. It can operate without a board of directors or formal bylaws.
4. It may establish its own mechanism for dispute resolution.

Although many close corporations are owned and managed by a small group of people or companies, their size can be as large as the largest public corporations.

Advantages of a Close Corporation

Closely held corporations have some advantages over publicly traded corporations. For example, a small, closely held corporation can make company-changing decisions much more quickly than a publicly traded company.

Disadvantages of a Close Corporation

Publicly traded companies have their own advantages over their closely held counterparts. Most notable is that publicly traded companies often have more working capital and can delegate debt throughout all shareholders.

Deciding Between a C or S Corporation

Typically, the S corporation status will benefit companies where the following apply:

- Shareholders work more than part time for the corporation.
- Shareholders have a firm grasp on the business and are familiar with the day-to-day business of the company.
- The corporation plans to distribute the majority of its profits to shareholders of the company each year.

A C corporation is better for companies whose employees are willing to take a low salary in order to leave the most money possible in the company in order to help it grow.

Limited Liability Company

A Limited Liability Company (LLC) is a hybrid business entity that has characteristics of both a corporation and a partnership. State laws governing LLCs vary greatly and should always be consulted. However, in most instances, the LLC is an attractive form of business organization for smaller companies with a single owner because it tends to allow greater flexibility in operation.

The primary corporate characteristic is that the LLC has the limited liability of a corporation and the partnership characteristic of passing through income taxation without the limitations of an S corporation.

Most states require an LLC to file a charter and an operating agreement. The charter contains the name and address of the company and other contact information while the operating agreement specifies the rights and obligations of the owners (members) of the company.

Under an LLC, members are not personally liable for the debts of the company and only risk their investment. However, they are liable for the consequences of their personal actions.

LLC Advantages

Limited liability companies are more flexible than other corporate forms, such as an S corporation, because they can have both corporate and partnership members. An LLC can also have different classes of stock, and it is not required to have annual meetings. In addition, LLC members may transfer their interests freely to anyone, but if the operating agreement is silent, members must obtain the unanimous permission of the all members before transferring their ownership rights. Although it depends on state law, most states permit the LLC to continue operating even after a member withdraws.

Disadvantages of an LLC

One of the major disadvantages of an LLC is that when it goes public, it loses its tax-free status and is taxed as a corporation, not a partnership. Thus, there is no advantage in being an LLC for publicly traded companies. Because of this and the fact that the law governing LLCs is not that stable and varies greatly among states, most privately held companies begin as LLCs and change to corporations when they go public.

Changing Form

If a company changes from a corporation to an LLC, the IRS treats the change as a sale of the corporate assets and taxes it accordingly. However, if a business changes from a partnership to an LLC or from an LLC to a corporation, it is not considered a sale and it will not have negative tax consequences for the business.

Hypothetical Case

Sally and Sam are expert Web site designers and decide to go into business together. Each of them has $10,000 they plan to contribute to starting up the business. They assume that after five years of hard work, they will be successful enough to hire other employees to do most of the work and they will merely manage the business. They already have a list of satisfied customers they have done work for and think they have several large corporations interested in contracting with them. They aren't sure what kind of business organization they should form, however, and ask you for advice. What information are you going to get from them, and how will that affect your advice?

Chapter 35
E-Commerce

Introduction

What is e-commerce? *E-commerce,* or electronic commerce, is the buying and selling of products and services through electronic means such as the Internet or any other electronic means. It encompasses a wide range of business activities:

- Electronic data interchange
- Automatic clearinghouse transactions
- Electronic mail
- Electronic support systems for products and/or customer support activities
- Electronic banking systems
- Ordering and material procurement support systems
- Inventory management systems
- Credit card and cash transactions

E-commerce occurs when one or more of the processes required to complete the business transaction is performed electronically or with the assistance of electronic tools. Many e-commerce activities are conducted on private networks, direct link telephone systems, the Internet, or other electronic mediums. E-commerce also includes all activities related to the business transaction, such as shopping, ordering, delivery, payment, and customer support functions.

Privacy Issues

Privacy is a collection of legal rights and issues having a common focus built around an individual's right to be free from observation by others in non-public places without their knowledge or consent. E-commerce has given rise to what has become known as *information privacy* issues.

Although U.S. courts have long recognized a person's right to keep private certain aspects of their personal conduct and what transpires in their own home, they have not been asked, until recently, to determine if a person has a legal right to control personal information about them. Unlike the courts in most European countries, the U.S. Supreme Court has ruled that an individual's control of personal information is not a fundamental right protected by the Fourteenth Amendment. This means that Web sites are free to collect information from visitors:

- Internet protocol (IP) address
- Browser, OS, hardware platform
- Browsing activity
- Time and date of visit
- URL of requested Web site
- URL of site from which request was made
- Responses to any questions or data fields

Also, unlike in Europe, in the U.S. there is no overall federal legislation on information privacy that regulates what commercial entities can do with the consumer information they collect. Instead, there are many federal statutes that deal with specific aspects of privacy in the context of e-commerce or other electronic activities. The U.S. approach to protecting information privacy is basically to let the market decide what is acceptable, at least for adults. However, although there is no legal requirement that Web sites have a privacy policy for the information they collect from users, most do. If a Web site has a privacy policy, the Federal Trade Commission (FTC) has oversight of them, and it has taken steps to regulate misrepresentations by Web sites. If a Web site's privacy policy states it does not or will not share user information with third parties, and it does so, the FTC may pursue litigation against them or obtain an informal resolution to the problem.

Children's Online Privacy Protection Act

The Children's Online Privacy Protection Act (COPPA) requires Web sites that target and solicit information from children under fourteen to obtain permission from a parent. This statute defines the characteristics of a Web site that targets children and contains specific requirements for how they can obtain and use information from them.

The Electronic Communications Privacy Act

The Electronic Communications Privacy Act (ECPA) outlaws the unauthorized interception of digital communications. The ECPA requires providers of public Internet communication services to keep the contents of communications (e-mail) confidential. However, it contains no such obligations regarding transactional records.

Gramm Leach Bliley Act—Financial Information Privacy

The Gramm Leach Bliley Act (GLBA), or the Financial Services Modernization Act, was intended to ease banking restrictions enacted after the Great Depression. It has recently been blamed for deregulating financial institutions to the point that another depression has been made possible. However, the GLBA also provides consumer privacy protections, which significantly impact the financial services industry and consumers.

The GLBA allows the integration of financial services. It authorizes banks, securities firms, and insurance companies to share personal customer information. Financial institutions must disclose to their customers who they share customer information with and for what purposes. This is an ongoing obligation that financial institutions must comply with at least once annually. In addition, consumers must be given the opportunity to "opt out" of the disclosure of their personal information by financial institutions.

Relevant Statutes

In addition to the statutes pertaining to privacy issues, there are several more that can impact e-commerce. Some of these are discussed next.

Communications Decency Act, Section 230

Section 230 of the Communications Decency Act (CDA) immunizes Internet service providers (ISP) who are "publishers" from any liability for any defamatory statements posted by third parties—even when the ISP purposefully solicits and advertises the postings knowing they are likely defamatory. As such, this statute significantly alters the traditional common law liability of publishers that media forms must follow. The rationale behind this change is that it would be too difficult for online publishers (meaning any Internet service provider that hosts a Web site) to police the content of all its contributors. While this is undoubtedly true, Section 230 has been criticized because it absolves ISPs from liability even when they knowingly publish defamatory information. As such, they have no motivation to remove defamatory content, even when advised of it. If a Web site makes statements about competitors or others or allows users to post comments, it should monitor them for defamatory content and remove such content, especially if notified of such.

The Computer Fraud and Abuse Act

The Computer Fraud and Abuse Act (CFAA) contains definitions of criminal fraud and abuse for federal computer crimes and removes the legal ambiguities and obstacles to prosecuting these crimes. The CFAA establishes felony offenses for the unauthorized access of "protected computers." It defines protected computers rather broadly, so that any computer that makes use of a financial system's site or a government site is a protected computer.

The CFAA makes it a crime to access any of the following without authorization:

- Information contained in a financial record of a financial institution, or of a card issuer or contained in a file of a consumer-reporting agency on a consumer, as such terms are defined in the Fair Credit Reporting Act
- Any information from any department or agency of the United States
- Information from any protected computer if the conduct involved an interstate or foreign communication

The CFAA also makes it a crime to knowingly do any of the following:

- Cause the transmission of a program that intentionally causes damage to a protected computer (virus, worm).
- Intentionally access a protected computer without authorization, and recklessly cause damage.
- Transmit in interstate or foreign commerce any communication containing any threat to cause damage to a protected computer.
- Use a computer to modify or impair the medical examination, medical diagnosis, medical treatment, or medical care of individuals.
- Use a computer to damage, or cause damage to, a computer, computer system, network, information, data, or program.

Security Issues

One of the most obvious concerns when conducting business, or any other transaction, electronically is determining the identity of the person you are dealing with. In electronic transactions, you cannot "see" who the other party is, so there must be a way to authenticate that others are who they say they are and verify their digital or electronic signature. Also, e-commerce requires a trustworthy computer system that provides confidentiality for information, contains access restrictions, and maintains information integrity by preventing its corruption or destruction while guaranteeing system availability. To do this, an e-commerce business must design a trustworthy computer system that provides for the following:

- Authentication
- Access control

- Integrity
- Audit
- Availability
- Secure login (i.e., PIN number or password)
- Digital signatures (i.e., an electronic signature produced through cryptography)

Other E-Commerce Concerns

In addition to the numerous statutes that impact e-commerce, a business that conducts transactions over the Internet also needs to be aware of and address a host of other issues.

Jurisdiction

Unlike bricks-and-mortar businesses, a business that operates on the Internet has no physical location that a person can identify. This is a problem, because the law has always based its jurisdictional requirements on where the parties are physically located. Thus, when a transaction occurs in "cyberspace," there is no location with obvious jurisdiction where litigation can be initiated. As a result, wise e-commerce entities will specify on their Web site where jurisdiction resides for any dispute resolution cases.

Intellectual Property

The advent of the Internet has had a huge impact on the area of intellectual property law. The ability and anonymity it provides people who post and copy intellectual property are enormous. It has never been easier to share music, photographs, and literary works. This had led to a huge increase in lawsuits for copyright violation and the creation or modification of laws dealing with it. Unfortunately, many Web site designers still don't realize that they cannot post someone else's intellectual property without the owner's explicit permission. The requirements for use of intellectual property are discussed in detail in that chapter, but suffice it to say here that any e-commerce site should contain only legally obtained and authorized intellectual property.

Tax Laws

As soon as states realized that a significant amount of merchandise was being sold over the Internet, they began efforts to obtain the sales tax revenue from those transactions. This meant they had to deal with a number of problems. Specifically, both customers and e-businesses wanted to avoid such payments and claimed the states had no jurisdiction over sales conducted on the Internet; it required a great deal of costly investment and monitoring ability on behalf of the e-business and the state; some businesses said the imposition of keeping track of and paying state sales tax would have a chilling effect on e-commerce, while bricks-and-mortar businesses said they were at a significant competitive disadvantage by having to pay taxes that e-businesses were able to avoid.

Today, most states require that people buying a product on the Internet pay sales tax on it. So far, the federal government has not instituted any federal tax for Internet sales or transactions but it is a reoccurring topic in Congress. Many large e-commerce sites do charge and collect sales tax based on where the customer geographically resides, and many states have passed laws that require their residents to voluntarily report their Internet purchases and pay taxes on them if it was not charged. Still, it remains quite common for e-commerce sites to refrain from charging sales tax on the products they sell.

E-Commerce Checklist

When creating a commercial Web site, be sure you have addressed the following areas:

- Jurisdiction
- Site security and the safety of any financial and user data
- Copyright, trademark, and patent
- State law governing electronic transactions
- Federal laws governing electronic transactions and data exchange/use
- Taxes
- Dispute settlement procedure
- Disclaimers
- Site use policies and procedures
- Privacy policy
- License and site access
- User account requirements
- Risk of loss
- Product descriptions
- Company's physical address

Hypothetical Case

Granada has a great idea for an online business. She plans to call her business "Granada's Great Gizmos." She has already sold over a hundred of her gizmos and anticipates she will sell thousands shortly after offering them for sale on the Internet. Currently, she and her younger brother buy the necessary parts and put the gizmos together in her basement, but she knows she'll have to hire more people and probably rent a manufacturing facility somewhere. She's already contracted with a Web design company to create her Web site, but she asks you for advice on what else she should do and what she should include on the Web site beyond the obvious description, as well as price and order information for gizmos. What questions are you going to ask Granada, and what advice are you going to give her?